Learn C# In One Day and Learn It Well
C# for Beginners with Hands-On Project
The only book you need to start coding in C# immediately

By Jamie Chan

http://www.learncodingfast.com/csharp

Preface

This book is written to help you learn C# FAST and learn it WELL.

The book does not assume any prior background in coding. If you are an absolute beginner, you'll find that this book explains complex concepts in an easy to understand manner. If you are an experienced coder but new to C#, this book will provide you with enough depth to start coding in C# immediately.

All examples in the book are carefully chosen to demonstrate each concept so that you can gain a deeper understanding of the language. Topics are carefully selected to give you a broad exposure to C#, while not overwhelming you with information overload. These topics include object-oriented programming concepts, error handling techniques, file handling techniques and more.

In addition, as Richard Branson puts it: "The best way of learning about anything is by doing". This book comes with a project where you'll be guided through the coding of a simple payroll software from scratch. The

project uses concepts covered in the book and gives you a chance to see how it all ties together.

You can download the source code for the project and all the sample programs in this book at
http://www.learncodingfast.com/csharp

Contact Information

I would love to hear from you.
For feedback or queries, you can contact me at
jamie@learncodingfast.com.

More Books by Jamie

Python: Learn Python in One Day and Learn It Well

Java: Learn Java in One Day and Learn It Well

CSS: Learn CSS in One Day and Learn It Well

Table of Contents

Chapter 1: Introduction to C#

Welcome to C# programming and thank you so much for picking up this book!

Whether you are a seasoned programmer or a complete novice, this book is written to help you learn C# programming fast. Topics are carefully selected to give you a broad exposure to C# while not overwhelming you with information overload.

By the end of the book, you should have no problem writing your own C# programs. In fact, we will be coding a simple payroll software together as part of the project at the end of the book. Ready to start?

First, let's answer a few questions:

What is C#?

C#, pronounced as C Sharp, is an object-oriented programming language developed by Microsoft in the early 2000s, led by Anders Hejlsberg. It is part of the .Net framework and is intended to be a simple general-purpose programming language that can be used to develop different types of applications, including console, windows, web and mobile applications.

Like all modern programming languages, C# code resembles the English language which computers are unable to understand. Therefore, C# code has to be converted into machine language using what is known as a compiler (*refer to footnote*). The compiler that we'll be using in this book is the free Visual Studio Community 2017 provided by Microsoft.

Why Learn C#?

C# has syntax and features that resemble other programming languages like Java and C++. As such, if you have any prior programming experience, you will find learning C# a breeze. Even if you are totally new to programming, C# is designed to be easy to learn (unlike C or C++) and is a great first language to learn.

In addition, C# is part of the .Net framework. This framework includes a large library of pre-written code that programmers can use without having to write everything from scratch. This allows programmers to rapidly develop their applications in C#, making C# the ideal language to work with if you are on a tight schedule.

Lastly, C# is an object-oriented programming (OOP) language. Object-oriented programming is an approach to programming that breaks a programming problem into objects that interact with each other. We'll be looking at various object-oriented programming concepts in this book. Once you master C#, you will be familiar with these concepts. This will make it easier for you to master other object-oriented programming languages in future.

Ready to dip your toes into the world of C# programming? Let's get started.

Footnote:
The conversion of a C# program into machine language is actually a bit more complicated than this. Visual Studio Community merely converts a C# program into MIL, which stands for Microsoft Intermediate Language. This MIL code is then converted into machine language by a virtual execution system known as the Common Language Runtime. For more information, you can check out https://msdn.microsoft.com/en-us/library/z1zx9t92.aspx. Nonetheless, for our purpose, we do not need to know these intricate details to develop our own C# programs.

Chapter 2: Getting ready for C#

Installing Visual Studio Community

Before we can start developing applications in C#, we need to download Visual Studio Community. As mentioned in Chapter 1, Visual Studio Community (VSC) is a free complier provided by Microsoft.

In fact, VSC is more than just a compiler. It is an Integrated Development Environment (IDE) that includes a text editor for us to write our code and a debugger to help us identify programming errors.

To download VSC, go to https://www.visualstudio.com/vs/community/.

Click on the "Download VS Community 2017" button to download the file. Once you have downloaded the file, double click to install VSC. You'll be presented with the screen below. Select ".Net desktop development" to proceed.

Once you finish installing the IDE, you are ready to start coding your first C# program.

Your First C# Program

To write our first program, let's create a folder on our desktop and name it "C# Projects". We will save all our C# projects to this folder.

Next, launch VSC and select File > New > Project.... (You may have to search for "Visual Studio 2017" if you cannot find VSC.) The first program that we are going to write is a console application. Console applications refer to programs that have no graphical user interface.

From the New Project dialog box, select "Visual C#" (on the left) and select "Console App (.Net Framework)" in the main box.

Name this program "HelloWorld" and save it in the "C# Projects" folder created earlier. You can use the "Browse..." button to browse to the correct folder. Finally, click OK to create the project.

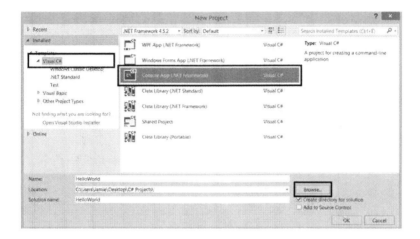

You will be presented with a default template that VSC created for you automatically.

Replace the code in the template with the code below. Note that line numbers are added for reference and are not part of the actual code. You may want to bookmark this page for easy reference later when we discuss the program. You can also download the source code for this sample program and all other sample programs in this book at http://www.learncodingfast.com/csharp.

```
1 using System;
2 using System.Collections.Generic;
3 using System.Linq;
4 using System.Text;
5 using System.Threading.Tasks;
```

```
6
7 namespace HelloWorld
8 {
9
10   //A Simple Program to display the words Hello
World
11
12   class Program
13   {
14       static void Main(string[] args)
15       {
16           Console.WriteLine("Hello World");
17           Console.Read();
18       }
19   }
20 }
```

I strongly encourage that you type the code yourself to get a better feel for how VSC works. As you type, you will notice that a box appears near the cursor with some help messages occasionally. That is known as Intellisense. For instance, when you type a period (.) after the word "Console", a dropdrop list appears to let you know what you can type after the period. This is one of the features of VSC to help make coding easier for programmers.

After you finish typing, you can execute this program by clicking on the "Start" button at the top menu (refer to image below).

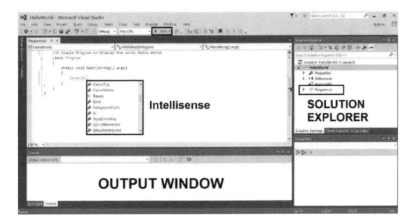

If your program fails to run, VSC will inform you of the error in the "Output Window". Double clicking on the error moves the cursor to where the error is. Double check your code against the code above to rectify the error and run the program again.

If all goes well and your program runs successfully, a black window will appear with the words "Hello World" in white. This black window is known as the console. Press Enter to close the window.

That's it! You have successfully coded your first program. Give yourself a pat on the shoulders.

If you navigate to your "C# Projects" folder now, you'll find a folder named "HelloWorld". Within the folder, you'll find another "HelloWorld" folder and a "HelloWorld.sln" file. This .sln file is the solution file. Whenever you need to reopen a project, this is the file to open. If the text editor does not display your code when you open the solution file, simply double click on the "Program.cs" file in the "Solution Explorer" on the right (refer to the previous image) to open it.

The executable file (.exe) of your code can be found in the HelloWorld > HelloWorld > bin > Debug folder.

Basic Structure of a C# Program

Now, let us do a quick run-through of the basic program that you have just coded.

Directive

From line 1 to 5, we have a few statements that start with the word using. These statements are known as directives. They tell the compiler that our program uses a certain namespace.

For instance, the first line

```
using System;
```

tells the compiler that our program uses the System namespace.

Namespace

A namespace is simply a grouping of related code elements. These elements include classes, interfaces, enums and structs etc (we'll cover each of these elements in subsequent chapters).

C# comes with a large amount of pre-written code that are organised into different namespaces. The `System` namespace contains code for methods that allow us to interact with our users. We use two of these methods in our program - the `WriteLine()` and `Read()` methods. The other namespaces are not needed in our program. However, since these namespaces are included in the default template, we'll leave it in our code.

In addition to the pre-written namespaces provided by Microsoft, we can also declare our own namespaces.

One advantage of declaring namespaces is that it prevents naming conflicts. Two or more code elements can have the same name as long as they belong to different namespaces. For instance, the code below defines two namespaces, both of which contain a class named `MyClass`. This is allowed in C# as the two classes belong to different namespaces (`First` and `Second`).

```
namespace First
{
    class MyClass
    {
    }
}

namespace Second
{
    class MyClass
    {
    }
}
```

In our example, we declared one namespace - `HelloWorld`.

The `HelloWorld` namespace starts on line 7, with an opening curly brace on line 8. It ends on line 20 with a closing curly brace. Curly braces are used extensively in C# to indicate the start and end of a code element. All opening braces in C# must be closed with a corresponding closing brace.

Within the `HelloWorld` namespace, we have the `Program` class which starts on line 12 and ends on line 19. Within the `Program` class, we have the `Main()` method that starts on line 14 and ends on line 18.

The Main() Method

The `Main()` method is the entry point of all C# console applications. Whenever a console application is started, the `Main()` method is the first method to be called.

In this book, whenever you are asked to try out a certain code segment, you should create a new "Console Application" and type the given code segment into the `Main()` method (between the curly braces). You can then run the program to test the code.

Notice the words "string[] args" inside the parenthesis of our `Main()` method? This means the `Main()` method can take in an array of strings as input. Do not worry about this for the moment. We'll cover these topics in subsequent chapters.

In our example, the `Main()` method contains two lines of code. The first line

```
Console.WriteLine("Hello World");
```

displays the line "Hello World" (without the quotes) on the screen.

The second line

```
Console.Read();
```

waits for a key press from the user before closing the window. You have to add this line to the end of the Main() method for all applications that you write in this book.

Both of the statements above end with a semi-colon. This is common for most statements in C#. After the `Console.Read()` statement, we end our code with three closing braces to close the earlier opening braces.

That's it! There's all there is to this simple program.

Comments

We've covered quite a bit in this chapter. You should now have a basic understanding of C# programming and be reasonably comfortable with VSC. Before we end this chapter, there's one more thing to learn - comments.

If you refer back to our "HelloWorld" example and look at line 10, you should notice that this line starts with two forward slashes (//).

```
//A Simple Program to display the words Hello World
```

This line is actually not part of the program. It is a comment that we write to make our code more readable for other programmers. Comments are ignored by the compiler.

To add comments to our program, we type two forward slashes (//) in front of each line of comment like this

```
// This is a comment
// This is another comment
// This is yet another comment
```

Alternatively, we can also use /* ... */ for multiline comments like this

```
/* This is a comment
This is also a comment
This is yet another comment
*/
```

Comments can also be placed after a statement, like this:

```
Console.Read();  //reads the next character
```

Chapter 3: The World of Variables and Operators

Now that you are familiar with VSC and have written your first program, let's get down to the real stuff. In this chapter, you'll learn all about variables and operators. Specifically, you'll learn what variables are and how to name, declare and initialize them. You'll also learn about the common operations that we can perform on them.

What are variables?

Variables are names given to data that we need to store and manipulate in our programs. For instance, suppose your program needs to store the age of a user. To do that, we can name this data `userAge` and declare the variable `userAge` using the following statement:

```
int userAge;
```

The declaration statement first states the data type of the variable, followed by its name. The data type of a variable refers to the type of data that the variable will store (such as whether it's a number or a piece of text). In our example, the data type is `int`, which refers to integers. The name of our variable is `userAge`.

After you declare the variable `userAge`, your program will allocate a certain area of your computer's storage space to store this data. You can then access and modify this data by referring to it by its name, `userAge`.

Data Types in C#

There are a number of commonly used data types in C#.

int

`int` stands for integer (i.e. numbers with no decimal or fractional parts) and holds numbers from -2,147,483,648 to 2,147,483,647. Examples include 15, 407, -908, 6150 etc.

byte

byte also refers to integral numbers, but has a narrower range from 0 to 255.

Most of the time, we use int instead of byte for integral numbers. However, if you are programming for a machine that has limited memory space, you should use byte if you are certain the value of the variable will not exceed the 0 to 255 range.

For instance, if you need to store the age of a user, you can use the byte data type as it is unlikely that the user's age will ever exceed 255 years old.

float

float refers to floating point numbers, which are numbers with decimal places such as 12.43, 5.2 and -9.12.

float can store numbers from -3.4×10^{38} to $+3.4 \times 10^{38}$. It uses 8 bytes of storage and has a precision of approximately 7 digits. This means that if you use float to store a number like 1.23456789 (10 digits), the number will be rounded off to 1.234568 (7 digits).

double

double is also a floating point number, but can store a much wider range of numbers. It can store numbers from $(+/-)5.0 \times 10^{-324}$ to $(+/-)1.7 \times 10^{308}$ and has a precision of about 15 to 16 digits.

double is the default floating point data type in C#. In other words, if you write a number like 2.34, C# treats it as a double by default.

decimal

decimal stores a decimal number but has a smaller range than float and double. However, it has a much greater precision of approximately 28-29 digits.

If your program requires a high degree of precision when storing non integral numbers, you should use a decimal data type. An example is when you are writing a financial application where precision is very important.

char

char stands for character and is used to store single Unicode characters such as 'A', '%', '@' and 'p' etc.

bool

bool stands for boolean and can only hold two values: true and false. It is commonly used in control flow statements. We'll cover control flow statements in Chapter 6.

Naming a Variable

A variable name in C# can only contain letters, numbers or underscores (_). However, the first character cannot be a number. Hence, you can name your variables userName, user_name or userName2 but not 2userName.

In addition, there are some reserved words that you cannot use as a variable name because they already have preassigned meanings in C#. These reserved words include words like Console, if, while etc. We'll learn about each of them in subsequent chapters.

Finally, variable names are case sensitive. username is not the same as userName.

There are two conventions when naming a variable in C#. We can either use the camel case notation or use underscores. Camel casing is the practice of writing compound words with mixed casing, capitalising the first letter of each word except the first word (e.g. `thisIsAVariableName`). This is the convention that we'll be using in the rest of the book. Alternatively, another common practice is to use underscores (_) to separate the words. If you prefer, you can name your variables like this: `this_is_a_variable_name`.

Initializing a Variable

Every time you declare a new variable, you need to give it an initial value. This is known as initializing the variable. You can change the value of the variable in your program later.

There are two ways to initialize a variable. You can initialize it at the point of declaration or initialize it in a separate statement.

The examples below show how you can initialize a variable at the point of declaration:

Example 1

These examples show how you can initialize `byte` and `int` variables.

```
byte userAge = 20;
int numberOfEmployees = 510;
```

As `byte` and `int` are for data with no decimal places, you will get an error if you write something like

```
byte userAge2 = 20.0;
```

20.0 is not the same as 20 in C#.

Example 2

The next examples show how you can initialize `double`, `float` and `decimal` variables with integral values. Although these data types are for numbers with decimal parts, we can also use them to store integral values as shown below.

```
double intNumberOfHours = 5120;
float intHourlyRate = 60;
decimal intIncome = 25399;
```

Example 3

The examples below show how you can initialize `double`, `float` and `decimal` variables with non integers.

```
double numberOfHours = 5120.5;
float hourlyRate = 60.5f;
decimal income = 25399.65m;
```

As mentioned previously, the default data type for a number with decimal places is `double`.

Hence, in the examples above, when you initialize `hourlyRate`, you need to add 'f' as a suffix after 60.5 to explicitly tell the complier to change 60.5 to a `float`.

Similarly, when you initialize `income`, you need to add 'm' as a suffix to change 25399.65 into a `decimal` data type.

Example 4

A `char` data type can only contain a single character. When we initialize a `char` variable, we need to enclose that character in single quotes. An example is:

```
char grade = 'A';
```

Example 5

A `bool` variable can only be either `true` or `false`. The example below shows how you can initialize a `bool` variable.

```
bool promote = true;
```

Example 6

In addition to initializing variables individually, you can also initialize multiple variables in the same statement as long as they are of the same data type. The following example shows how this can be done. Note that the two variables are separated with a comma and the statement ends with a semi-colon.

```
byte level = 2, userExperience = 5;
```

The six examples above show how you can initialize a variable at the point of declaration. Alternatively, you can choose to initialize a variable in a separate statement. An example is shown below:

```
byte year;   //declare the variable
year = 20;   //initialize it
```

The Assignment Sign

The = sign in programming has a different meaning from the = sign we learned in Math. In programming, the = sign is known as an assignment sign. It means we are assigning the value on the right side of the = sign to the variable on the left. A good way to understand a statement like `year = 20` is to think of it as `year <- 20`.

In programming, the statements `x = y` and `y = x` have very different meanings.

Confused? An example will likely clear this up.

Suppose we have two variables `x` and `y` and

```
x = 5; y = 10;
```

If you write

```
x = y;
```

your Math teacher is probably going to be upset at you since x is not equal to y.

However, in programming, this is fine. This statement means we are assigning the value of y to x (think of it as x <- y). It is alright to assign the value of a variable to another variable. In our example, the value of x is now changed to 10 while the value of y remains unchanged. In other words, x = 10 and y = 10 now.

Now suppose we change the values of x and y back to

```
x = 5; y = 10;
```

If you now write

```
y = x;
```

it means you are assigning the value of x to y (think of it as y <- x). Mathematically, $x = y$ and $y = x$ mean the same thing. However, this is not so in programming. Here, the value of y is changed to 5 while the value of x remains unchanged. In other words, x = 5 and y = 5 now.

Basic Operators

Besides assigning an initial value to a variable or assigning another variable to it, we can also perform the usual mathematical operations on variables. Basic operators in C# include +, -, *, / and % which represent addition, subtraction, multiplication, division and modulus respectively.

Example

Suppose x = 7, y = 2

Addition:	x + y = 9
Subtraction:	x - y = 5
Multiplication:	x*y = 14
Division:	x/y = 3 (rounds down the answer to the nearest integer)
Modulus:	x%y = 1 (gives the remainder when 7 is divided by 2)

In C#, division gives an integer answer if both x and y are integers. However, if either x or y is a non integer, we will get a non integer answer. For instance,

7 / 2 = 3
7.0 / 2 = 3.5
7 / 2.0 = 3.5
7.0 / 2.0 = 3.5

In the first case, when an integer is divided by another integer, you get an integer as the answer. The decimal portion of the answer, if any, is truncated. Hence, we get 3 instead of 3.5.

In all other cases, the result is a non integer as at least one of the operands is a non integer.

More Assignment Operators

Besides the = sign, there are a few more assignment operators in C# (and most programming languages). These include operators like +=, -= and *=.

Suppose we have the variable x, with an initial value of 10. If we want to increment x by 2, we can write

```
x = x + 2;
```

The program will first evaluate the expression on the right (x + 2) and assign the answer to the left. So eventually the statement above becomes x <- 12.

Instead of writing x = x + 2, we can also write x += 2 to express the same meaning. The += sign is actually a shorthand that combines the assignment sign with the addition operator. Hence, x += 2 simply means x = x + 2.

Similarly, if we want to do a subtraction, we can write x = x - 2 or `x -= 2`. The same works for all the 5 operators mentioned in the section above.

Most programming languages also have the `++` and `--` operators. The `++` operator is used when you want to increase the value of a variable by 1. For instance, suppose

```
int x = 2;
```

If you write

```
x++;
```

the value of x becomes 3.

There is no need to use the `=` sign when you use the `++` operator. The statement `x++;` is equivalent to

```
x = x + 1;
```

The `++` operator can be placed in front of or behind the variable name. This affects the order in which tasks are performed.

Suppose we have an integer named `counter`. If we write

```
Console.WriteLine(counter++);
```

the program first prints the original value of `counter` before incrementing `counter` by 1. In other words, it executes the tasks in this order

```
Console.WriteLine(counter);
counter = counter + 1;
```

On the other hand, if we write

```
Console.WriteLine(++counter);
```

the program first increments `counter` by 1 before printing the new value of `counter`. In other words, it executes the tasks in this order

```
counter = counter + 1;
Console.WriteLine(counter);
```

In addition to the `++` operator, we also have the `--` operator (two minus signs). This operator decreases the value of the variable by 1.

Type Casting In C#

Sometimes in our program, it is necessary to convert from one data type to another, such as from a `double` to an `int`. This is known as type casting.

To convert one numeric data type to another, we just need to add `(new data type)` in front of the data that we want to convert.

For instance, we can cast a non integer into an integer like this:

```
int x = (int) 20.9;
```

When we cast 20.9 into an integer, the resulting value is 20, not 21. The decimal portion is truncated after the conversion.

We can also cast a `double` into a `float` or a `decimal`. Recall that we mentioned earlier that all non integers are treated as `double` by default in C#? If we want to assign a number like 20.9 to a `float` or `decimal`, we need to add the 'f' and 'm' suffixes respectively. Another way to do it is to use a cast, like this:

```
float num1 = (float) 20.9;
decimal num2 = (decimal) 20.9;
```

The values of `num1` and `num2` will both be 20.9.

In addition to casting between numeric types, we can also do other types of casting. We'll explore some of these conversions in subsequent chapters.

Chapter 4: Arrays, Strings and Lists

In the previous chapter, we covered some of the basic data types that are commonly used in C#. Besides these basic data types, C# also comes with a few advanced data types. In this chapter, we are going to cover three advanced data types: arrays, strings and lists. In addition, we are going to discuss the difference between a value data type and a reference data type.

Array

An array is simply a collection of data that are normally related to each other. Suppose we want to store the ages of 5 users. Instead of storing them as `user1Age`, `user2Age`, `user3Age`, `user4Age` and `user5Age`, we can store them as an array.

An array can be declared and initialized as follows:

```
int[] userAge = {21, 22, 23, 24, 25};
```

`int` indicates that this variable stores `int` values.
`[]` indicates that the variable is an array instead of a normal variable.
`userAge` is the name of the array.
`{21, 22, 23, 24, 25}` are the five integers that the array stores.

In addition to declaring and initializing an array at the point of declaration, we can declare an array first and initialize it later. To do that, we need to use the `new` operator:

```
int[] userAge2;
userAge2 = new [] {21, 22, 23, 24, 25};
```

The first statement declares the array. The second statement initializes it with the integers 21, 22, 23, 24 and 25.

Finally, we can also declare an array and initialize it with default values. To do that, we write:

```
int[] userAge3 = new int[5];
```

This statement declares an array of 5 integers (as indicated by the number 5 inside the square brackets [ ]). As we did not specify the values of these 5 integers, C# automatically initializes them to the default value. The default value for integers is 0. Hence, the array becomes {0, 0, 0, 0, 0}.

You can update the individual values in the array by accessing them using their indexes. Indexes always start with a value of ZERO, not 1. This is a common practice in almost all programming languages, such as Python and Java. The first value of the array has an index of 0, the next has an index of 1 and so forth. Supposed the array userAge is currently {21, 22, 23, 24, 25}. To update the first value of the array, we write

```
userAge[0] = 31;
```

the array becomes {31, 22, 23, 24, 25}.

If we type

```
userAge[2] = userAge[2] + 20;
```

the array becomes {31, 22, 43, 24, 25}. That is, 20 is added to the third element.

Array Properties and Methods

C# comes with a number of useful properties and methods that we can use with an array.

We'll learn more about properties and methods in Chapter 7 when we discuss classes. For now, all we have to know is that to use a property or method, we need to use the dot (.) operator. To use a property, we type the property name after the dot. To use a method, we type the method name after the dot operator, followed by a pair of parenthesis ().

Length

The `Length` property of an array tells us the number of items the array has.

For instance, if we have

```
int [] userAge = {21, 22, 26, 32, 40};
```

`userAge.Length` is equal to 5 as there are 5 numbers in the array.

Copy()

The `Copy()` method allows you to copy the contents of one array into another array, starting from the first element.

In C#, a method may have many different variations. For instance, the `Copy()` method comes in four different variations. The example below discusses one of the four variations. If you learn how to use one variation, you can figure out how to use the other `Copy()` methods with relative ease.

Whenever we use a method, we need to put a pair of parenthesis () after the method name. Some methods require certain data for it to work. These data are known as arguments. We include these arguments in the pair of parenthesis. The `Copy()` method requires three arguments.

Suppose you have

```
int [] source = {12, 1, 5, -2, 16, 14};
```

and

```
int [] dest = {1, 2, 3, 4};
```

You can copy the first three elements of `source` into `dest` by using the statement below:

```
Array.Copy(source, dest, 3);
```

The first argument is the array that provides the values to be copied. The second is the array where the values will be copied into. The last argument specifies the number of items to copy.

In our example, our `dest` array becomes {12, 1, 5, 4} while the `source` array remains unchanged.

Sort()

The `Sort()` method allows us to sort our arrays. It takes in an array as the argument.

Suppose you have

```
int [] numbers = {12, 1, 5, -2, 16, 14};
```

You can sort this array by writing

```
Array.Sort(numbers);
```

The array will be sorted in ascending order. Thus, `numbers` becomes {-2, 1, 5, 12, 14, 16}.

IndexOf()

We use the `IndexOf()` method to determine if a certain value exists in an array. If it exists, the method returns the index of the first occurrence of that value. If it does not exist, the method returns -1.

For instance, if you have

```
int [] numbers = {10, 30, 44, 21, 51, 21, 61, 24, 14};
```

you can find if the value 21 exists in the array by writing

```
Array.IndexOf(numbers, 21);
```

The method returns the index of the first value found, which is 3 in this case since 21 is the fourth element in the array. You can then assign the answer to a variable like this:

```
int ans = Array.IndexOf(numbers, 21);
```

The value of `ans` is thus 3. If you write

```
ans = Array.IndexOf(numbers, 100);
```

the value of `ans` is -1 as 100 does not exist in the `numbers` array.

We've covered some of the more commonly used array methods in this section. For a complete list of all the array methods available in C#, check out this page https://msdn.microsoft.com/en-us/library/system.array_methods(v=vs.110).aspx

String

Next, let us look at the `string` data type. A string is a piece of text. An example of a string is the text "Hello World".

To declare and initialize a `string` variable, you write

```
string message = "Hello World";
```

where `message` is the name of the `string` variable and "Hello World" is the string assigned to it. Note that you need to enclose the string in double quotes (").

You can also assign an empty string to a variable, like this:

```
string anotherMessage = "";
```

Finally, we can join two or more strings using the concatenate sign (+) and assign them to a variable. For instance, we can write

```
string myName = "Hello World, " + "my name is Jamie";
```

This is the same as

```
string myName = "Hello World, my name is Jamie";
```

String Properties and Methods

Like arrays, strings come with a number of properties and methods.

Length

The `Length` property of a string tells us the total number of characters the string contains.

To find the length of the string "Hello World", we write
`"Hello World".Length`

We will get the value 11 as "Hello" and "World" both have 5 characters each. When you add the space between the two words, you get a total length of 11.

Substring()

The `Substring()` method is used to extract a substring from a longer string.

It requires two arguments. The first tells the compiler the index of the starting position to extract and the second tells the compiler the length.

Suppose we declare a `string` variable `message` and assign the string "Hello World" to it.

```
string message = "Hello World";
```

We can then use `message` to call the `Substring()` method as shown below.

```
string newMessage = message.Substring(2, 5);
```

`Substring(2, 5)` extracts a substring of 5 characters from `message`, starting from index 2 (which is the third letter as indexes always start from 0).

The resulting substring is then assigned to `newMessage`.

`newMessage` is thus equal to "llo W".

`message`, on the other hand, is not changed. It remains as "Hello World".

Equals()

We can use the `Equals()` method to compare if two strings are identical.

If we have two strings as shown below
```
string firstString = "This is Jamie";
string secondString = "Hello";
```

```
firstString.Equals("This is Jamie");
```

returns `true` while

```
firstString.Equals(secondString);
```

returns `false` as the two strings (`firstString` and `secondString`) are not equal.

Split()

The `Split()` method splits a string into substrings based on an array of user-defined separators. After splitting the string, the `Split()` method returns an array that contains the resulting substrings.

The `Split()` method requires two arguments - an array of strings that act as separators and a second argument to specify whether you want to remove empty strings from the result.

Suppose you want to split the string "Peter, John; Andy, ,David" into substrings, you can do it as follows (line numbers are added for reference):

```
1 string [] separator = {", ", "; "};
2 string names = "Peter, John; Andy, , David";
3 string [] substrings = names.Split(separator,
StringSplitOptions.None);
```

On Line 1, we first declare an array of two strings to act as separators. The first string is a comma followed by a space and the second is a semi-colon followed by a space.

On Line 2, we assign the string that we want to split to the `names` variable. On Line 3, we use the `names` variable to call the `Split()` method and assign its result to the `substrings` array.

The result of the code above is the following array
```
{"Peter", "John", "Andy", "" , "David"}
```

This array contains an empty string as there is a space between the comma after "Andy" and the comma before "David" in the original string. If you want to remove the empty string from the result, you have to change Line 3 to

```
string [] substrings = names.Split(separator,
StringSplitOptions.RemoveEmptyEntries);
```

The `substrings` array thus becomes

```
{"Peter", "John", "Andy", "David"}
```

As usual, we've only covered a number of the more commonly used string methods. For a complete list of all the string methods available in C#, check out this page https://msdn.microsoft.com/en-us/library/system.string_methods(v=vs.110).aspx

Lists

Now, let us look at the last data type in this chapter – lists. A list stores values like an array, but elements can be added or removed at will.

An array can only hold a fixed number of values. If you declare

```
int [] myArray = new int[10];
```

myArray can only hold 10 values. If you write myArray[10] (which refers to the 11th value since array index starts from zero), you will get an error.

If you need greater flexibility in your program, you can use a list.

To declare a list of integers, we write

```
List<int> userAgeList = new List<int>();
```
userAgeList is the name of the list.
List is a keyword to indicate that you are declaring a list.
The data type is enclosed in angle brackets < >.

You can choose to initialize the list at the point of declaration like this

```
List<int> userAgeList = new List<int> {11, 21, 31,
41};
```

To access the individual elements in a list, we use the same notation as when we access elements in an array. For instance, to access the first element, you write userAgeList[0]. To access the third element, you write userAgeList[2].

List Properties and Methods

The list data type also comes with a large number of properties and methods.

Add()

You can add members to a list using the Add() method.

```
userAgeList.Add(51);
userAgeList.Add(61);
```

userAgeList now has 6 members: {11, 21, 31, 41, 51, 61}.

Count

To find out the number of elements in the list, use the `Count` property.
`userAgeList.Count` gives us 6 as there are 6 elements in the list at
the moment.

Insert()

To add members at a specific position, use the `Insert()` method.

To insert a member at the 3rd position, you write

`userAgeList.Insert(2, 51);`

where 2 is the index and 51 is the value you want to insert.

`userAgeList` now becomes `{11, 21, 51, 31, 41, 51, 61}`.

Remove()

To remove members from the list, use the `Remove()` method. The
`Remove()` method takes in one argument and removes the first
occurrence of that argument. For instance, if we write

`userAgeList.Remove(51);`

`userAgeList` becomes `{11, 21, 31, 41, 51, 61}`. Only the first
'51' is removed.

RemoveAt()

To remove a member at a specific location, use the `RemoveAt()`
method. For instance, to remove the 4th item (index 3), you write

`userAgeList.RemoveAt(3);`

where 3 is the index of the item to be removed.

`userAgeList` now becomes `{11, 21, 31, 51, 61}`.

Contains()

To check if a list contains a certain member, use the `Contains()` method.

To check if `userAgeList` contains '51', we write

```
userAgeList.Contains(51);
```

We will get `true` as the result.

Clear()

To remove all items in a list, use the `Clear()` method. If we write

```
userAgeList.Clear();
```

we will have no elements left in the list.

For a complete list of all the list methods available in C#, check out this page https://msdn.microsoft.com/en-us/library/s6hkc2c4(v=vs.110).aspx

Value Type vs. Reference Type

Now that we are familiar with strings, arrays and lists, let us discuss an important concept regarding data types in C#.

All data types in C# can be classified as either a value type or a reference type. The data types discussed in Chapter 3 are value types. Those discussed in this chapter are reference types.

A value data type is a variable that stores its own data.

When we write

```
int myNumber = 5;
```

the variable `myNumber` stores the actual value 5.

A reference type, on the other hand, does not store the actual data. Instead, it stores a reference to the data. It does not tell the compiler what the value of the data is; it tells the compiler where to find the actual data.

An example of a reference type is a `string`. When you write a statement like

```
string message = "Hello";
```

the variable `message` actually does not store the string "Hello". Instead, the string "Hello" is created and stored elsewhere in the computer's memory. The variable `message` stores the address of that memory location.

That's all that we need to know about reference types at the moment. As this is a book for beginners, we will not go into details about why reference types are necessary. Just be aware that there is a difference between value types and reference types; the former stores a value while the latter stores an address.

Chapter 5: Making our Program Interactive

Now that we have covered the basics of variables and data types, let us write a program that makes use of them. In this chapter, we'll learn how to accept input from users, store the data in a variable and display messages to our users. Ready?

Displaying Messages to Users

To display messages to our users, we use the `Write()` or `WriteLine()` method provided by C#, available in the `System` namespace.

The difference between `WriteLine()` and `Write()` is that `Writeline()` moves the cursor down to the next line after displaying the message while `Write()` does not.

If we write

```
Console.WriteLine("Hello ");
Console.WriteLine("How are you?");
```

we'll get

```
Hello
How are you?
```

If we write

```
Console.Write("Hello ");
Console.Write("How are you?");
```

we'll get

```
Hello How are you?
```

Note that in the examples above, we added the word `Console` in front of the method name whenever we call the `WriteLine()` or `Write()`

method. This is because both methods are static methods of the `Console` class. We'll talk more about static methods in Chapter 7.

If you find it troublesome to add the word `Console` whenever you use these two methods, you can add the directive

```
using static System.Console;
```

to the start of your program. If you do that, you can simply write

```
WriteLine("Hello World");
```

instead of

```
Console.WriteLine("Hellow World");
```

whenever you use any of the static methods in the `Console` class. This is a new feature in C# 6 (the latest version of C#) and is available only if you use the latest IDE (i.e. Visual Studio 2017). For the rest of our examples, we'll stick to the first method for backwards compatibility.

We have already seen an example of how we can use the `WriteLine()` method when we wrote the "Hello World" program in Chapter 2. Let us now look at more examples. In the examples below, we'll focus on the `WriteLine()` method. The `Write()` method works exactly the same way.

Example 1

To display a simple string, we write

```
Console.WriteLine("Hello, how are you?");
```

Output

```
Hello, how are you?
```

Example 2

To display the value of a variable, we pass in the variable name as an argument. For instance, suppose we have

```
int userAge = 30;
```

we display the value of `userAge` by writing

```
Console.WriteLine(userAge);
```

Output

```
30
```

Note that we do not enclose the variable name (`userAge`) in double quotes. If we write

```
Console.WriteLine("userAge");
```

we'll get

```
userAge
```

as the output instead.

Example 3

To combine two or more strings and display them, we use the concatenation (+) sign mentioned in the previous chapter.

For instance, if we write

```
Console.WriteLine("Hello, " + "how are you?" + " I
love C#.");
```

we'll get

```
Hello, how are you? I love C#.
```

Example 4

We can also use the concatenation sign to combine a string and a variable. Suppose we have

```
int results = 79;
```

The statement

```
Console.WriteLine("You scored " + results + " marks
for your test.");
```

gives us

```
You scored 79 marks for your test.
```

Again, we do not enclose the variable name in double quotes. Else we will get

```
You scored results marks for your test.
```

Example 5

In addition to using the concatenation sign to combine strings and variables, we can use placeholders. Suppose we have

```
int results = 79;
```

If we write

```
Console.WriteLine("{0}! You scored {1} marks for your
test.", "Good morning", results);
```

we will get

```
Good morning! You scored 79 marks for your test.
```

In this example, we passed in three arguments to the `WriteLine()` method, separated by commas.

The three arguments are

1) `"{0}! You scored {1} marks for your test."`
2) `"Good morning"`
3) `results`

The first is the string that will be displayed. Within the string, the curly braces act as placeholders and will be replaced by the arguments that follow.

`{0}` is a placeholder for the next argument, which is the string "Good morning" in this case.

`{1}` is a placeholder for the variable `results`.
Therefore the output is

```
Good morning! You scored 79 marks for your test.
```

If you wrote

```
Console.WriteLine("{1}! You scored {0} marks for your test.", "Good morning", results);
```

you'll get

```
79! You scored Good morning marks for your test.
```

Of course, such a statement makes no sense. However, it demonstrates how placeholders are replaced by the corresponding arguments.

We can specify how we want numeric values to be displayed when using placeholders. This is done using a format specifier, such as the `C` and `F` specifiers.

The `F` specifier specifies the number of decimal places a number should be displayed with.

If we write

```
Console.WriteLine("The number is {0:F3}.",
123.45678);
```

we'll get

```
The number is 123.457.
```

The F3 specifier rounds the number 123.45678 off to 123.457. Note that there should not be any space before the specifier. In other words, it has to be {0:F3} and not {0: F3}.

The C specifier is for formatting currencies; it adds the "$" symbol in front of the number and displays the number with 2 decimal places. In addition, it separates every thousand with a comma.

If you write

```
Console.WriteLine("Deposit = {0:C}. Account balance =
{1:C}.", 2125, 12345.678);
```

you'll get

```
Deposit = $2,125.00. Account balance = $12,345.68
```

Example 6

We can also use Console.WriteLine() to print the result of a method.

In Chapter 4, we learned how to use the Substring() method to extract a substring from a longer string. In that example, we assigned the result to another string. Alternatively, we can use Console.WriteLine() to display the result without assigning it a variable.

For instance, if you write

```
Console.WriteLine("Microsoft".Substring(1, 3));
```

The output

```
icr
```

will be displayed on the screen.

Besides displaying the result of a method, `Console.WriteLine()` can also be used to display the value of a property. If we write

```
Console.WriteLine("Hello World".Length);
```

the value

```
11
```

will be displayed on the screen.

Escape Sequences

Sometimes in our programs, we may need to print some special "unprintable" characters such as a tab or a newline. In this case, you need to use the \ (backslash) character to escape characters that otherwise have a different meaning.

For instance to print a tab, we type the backslash character before the letter t, like this: `\t`.

Without the \ character, the letter "t" will be printed. With it, a tab is printed. Hence, if you type

```
Console.WriteLine("Hello\tWorld");
```

you'll get

```
Hello    World
```

Other common uses of the backslash character include:

To prints a newline (\n)

Example

```
Console.WriteLine("Hello\nWorld");
```

Output

```
Hello
World
```

To print the backslash character itself (\\)

Example

```
Console.WriteLine("\\");
```

Output

```
\
```

To print double quotes (\") so that the double quote does not end the string

Example

```
Console.WriteLine("I am 5'9\" tall");
```

Output

```
I am 5'9" tall
```

Accepting User Input

Now that we know how to display messages to our users, let us look at how we can accept input from them.

To accept user input, we can use either the `Read()` or `ReadLine()` method.

`Read()` reads the next character from standard input while `ReadLine()` reads a line of characters. Standard input refers to the standard device that users use to enter data, which is usually the keyboard.

The example below shows how we can use the `ReadLine()` method to read input from users. The `Read()` method works the same way.

```
string userInput = Console.ReadLine();
```

Both the `Read()` and `ReadLine()` methods read in user input as a **string**. Hence, in the example above, we assign the result of `Console.ReadLine()` to a `string` variable called `userInput`.

We can then use

```
Console.WriteLine(userInput);
```

to print out the input that the user entered.

Converting a String to a Number

Sometimes, it is necessary to convert the input that users entered into a numeric data type so that you can perform calculations on it. C# provides us with a number of methods to do the conversion. The methods that we use are found in the `Convert` class, which is also grouped under the `System` namespace.

To convert a string to an integer, we use the `ToInt32()` method. For instance, if we have

```
string userInput = Console.ReadLine();
```

and the user keys in 20, `userInput` will be equal to "20" (which is a string and not an integer because of the double quotes).

We can then use

```
int newUserInput = Convert.ToInt32(userInput);
```

to convert the string to the integer 20 and assign it to an `int` variable. We can now perform the usual mathematical operations on this new `int` variable.

Besides converting a string to an integer, we can also convert a string to a `decimal`, `float` or `double` using the `ToDecimal()`, `ToSingle()` and `ToDouble()` methods respectively.

Putting it all Together

Now let us put everything that we've learned together to write a complete program. We'll modify the "Hello World" program that we wrote in Chapter 2. Instead of just saying hello to the world, we want the world to know our names and ages too.

First, fire up Visual Studio Community and create a new Visual C# Console Application project. Name the project "HelloWorldAgain".

Type the following code segment into the `Main()` method (line numbers are added for reference).

```
1   string userName = "";
2   int userAge = 0;
3   int currentYear = 0;
4
5   Console.Write("Please enter your name: ");
6   userName = Console.ReadLine();
7   Console.Write("Please enter your age: ");
8   userAge = Convert.ToInt32(Console.ReadLine());
9   Console.Write("Please enter the current year: ");
10  currentYear = Convert.ToInt32(Console.ReadLine());
11
12  Console.WriteLine("Hello World! My name is {0} and
I am {1} years old. I was born in {2}.", userName,
userAge, currentYear - userAge);
```

Run the program and enter the following information

```
Please enter your name: Jamie
```

```
Please enter your age: 39
Please enter the current year: 2015
```

The program should give you the following output

```
Hello World! My name is Jamie and I am 39 years old.
I was born in 1976.
```

This program should be quite easy to understand. However, there are two points to mention about the program.

Firstly, Line 10 shows an example of how we can use two methods within the same statement. When we write

```
userAge = Convert.ToInt32(Console.ReadLine());
```

the `Console.ReadLine()` method is executed first as it is within a pair of parenthesis (). This is similar to how operations within parenthesis have a higher order of precedence when we evaluate a mathematical expression. For instance, when we evaluate 3 * (5 + 9), we have to add 5 to 9 first before multiplying the answer to 3 (i.e. 3*14).

After `Console.ReadLine()` is executed, the value entered by the user is converted to an integer using `Convert.ToInt32()`.

Suppose the user entered 39.

```
Convert.ToInt32(Console.ReadLine())
```

becomes

```
Convert.ToInt32("39").
```

The result of `Convert.ToInt32("39")` is the integer 39. This integer is then assigned to variable `userAge`.

The next thing to point out about the program is Line 12 as shown below:

```
Console.WriteLine("Hello World! My name is {0} and I
am {1} years old. I was born in {2}.", userName,
userAge, currentYear - userAge);
```

Notice that the last argument (`currentYear - userAge`) involves a Mathematical operation? This is allowed in C#. `WriteLine()` will perform the subtraction and display the result of the calculation.

Chapter 6: Making Choices and Decisions

Congratulations on making it thus far. We've come a long way. You now know the different data types in C# and are able to code a simple program that interacts with users.

In this chapter, we are going to cover another fundamental concept in programming; we'll learn how to control the flow of a program using control flow statements.

Specifically, we will learn about the `if` statement, the inline `if` statement, the `switch` statement, the `for` loop, the `foreach` loop, the `while` loop and the `do while` loop. In addition, we will also learn about the `try-catch-finally` statement that controls the flow of the program when an error occurs.

However, before we go into these control tools, we have to first look at condition statements.

Condition Statements

Most control flow statements involve evaluating a condition statement. The program will proceed differently depending on whether the condition is met.

The most common condition statement is the comparison statement. If we want to compare whether two variables are the same, we use the `==` sign (double =). For instance, if you write `x == y`, you are asking the program to check if the value of `x` is equal to the value of `y`. If they are equal, the condition is met and the statement evaluates to `true`. Else, the statement evaluates to `false`.

In addition to evaluating whether one value is equal to another, there are other comparison operators that we can use in our condition statements.

Not equal (!=)

Returns `true` if the left is not equal to the right

```
5 != 2 is true
6 != 6 is false
```

Greater than (>)

Returns `true` if the left is greater than the right

```
5 > 2 is true
3 > 6 is false
```

Smaller than (<)

Returns `true` if the left is smaller than the right

```
1 < 7 is true
9 < 6 is false
```

Greater than or equal to (>=)

Returns `true` if the left is greater than or equal to the right

```
5 >= 2 is true
5 >= 5 is true
3 >= 6 is false
```

Smaller than or equal to (<=)

Returns `true` if the left is smaller than or equal to the right

```
11 <= 7 is true
7 <= 7 is true
9 <= 6 is false
```

We also have three logical operators (`&&`, `||`, `!`) that are useful if we want to combine multiple conditions.

The AND operator (&&)

Returns `true` if **all** conditions are met

`5==5 && 2>1 && 3!=7` is true
`5==5 && 2<1 && 3!=7` is false as the second condition (`2<1`) is false

The OR operator (||)

Returns `true` if **at least one** condition is met.

`5==5 || 2<1 || 3==7` is true as the first condition (`5==5`) is true
`5==6 || 2<1 || 3==7` is false as all conditions are false

Control Flow Statements

Now that we are familiar with condition statements, let us proceed to learn how we can use these statements to control the flow of a program.

If Statement

The `if` statement is one of the most commonly used control flow statements. It allows the program to evaluate if a certain condition is met, and to perform the appropriate action based on the result of the evaluation. The structure of an `if` statement is as follows (line numbers are added for reference):

```
1    if (condition 1 is met)
2    {
3         do Task A
4    }
5    else if (condition 2 is met)
6    {
7         do Task B
8    }
9    else if (condition 3 is met)
10   {
11        do Task C
12   }
13   else
14   {
15        do Task E
```

```
16  }
```

Line 1 tests the first condition. If the condition is met, everything inside the pair of curly braces that follow (lines 2 to 4) will be executed. The rest of the `if` statement (from line 5 to 16) will be skipped.

If the first condition is not met, you can use the `else if` statements that follow to test more conditions (lines 5 to 12). There can be multiple `else if` statements. Finally, you can use the `else` statement (lines 13 to 16) to execute some code if none of the preceding conditions are met.
To fully understand how the `if` statement works, add the following code to the `Main()` program in the VSC template.

```
int userAge;

Console.Write("Please enter your age: ");
userAge = Convert.ToInt32(Console.ReadLine());

if (userAge < 0 || userAge > 100)
{
    Console.WriteLine("Invalid Age");
    Console.WriteLine("Age must be between 0 and
100");
}
else if (userAge < 18)
    Console.WriteLine("Sorry you are underage");
else if (userAge < 21)
    Console.WriteLine("You need parental consent");
else
{
    Console.WriteLine("Congratulations!");
    Console.WriteLine("You may sign up for the
event!");
}
```

The program first prompts the user for his age and stores the result in the `userAge` variable.

Next the statement

```
if (userAge < 0 || userAge > 100)
```

checks if the value of `userAge` is smaller than zero or greater than 100. If either of the conditions is `true`, the program will execute all statements within the curly braces that follow. In this example, it'll print "Invalid Age", followed by "Age must be between 0 and 100".

On the other hand, if both conditions are `false`, the program will test the next condition - `else if (userAge < 18)`. If `userAge` is less than 18 (but more than or equal to 0 since the first condition is not met), the program will print "Sorry you are underage".

You may notice that we did not enclose the statement

```
Console.WriteLine("Sorry you are underage");
```

in curly braces. This is because curly braces are optional if there is only one statement to execute.

If the user did not enter a value smaller than 18, but entered a value greater than or equal to 18 but smaller than 21, the next `else if` statement will be executed. In this case, the message "You need parental consent" will be printed.

Finally, if the user entered a value greater than or equal to 21 but smaller than or equal to 100, the program will execute the code in the `else` block. In this case, it will print "Congratulations" followed by "You may sign up for the event!".

Run the program five times and enter -1, 8, 20, 23 and 121 respectively for each run. You'll get the following outputs:

```
Please enter your age: -1
Invalid Age
Age must be between 0 and 100

Please enter your age: 8
Sorry you are underage
Please enter your age: 20
You need parental consent
```

```
Please enter your age: 23
Congratulations!
You may sign up for the event!

Please enter your age: 121
Invalid Age
Age must be between 0 and 100
```

Inline If

An inline `if` statement is a simpler form of an `if` statement that is very convenient if you want to assign a value to a variable depending on the result of a condition. The syntax is:

```
condition ? value if condition is true : value if
condition is false;
```

For instance, the statement

```
3>2 ? 10 : 5;
```

returns the value 10 since 3 is greater than 2 (i.e. the condition $3 > 2$ is true). This value can then be assigned to a variable.

If we write

```
int myNum = 3>2 ? 10 : 5;
```

`myNum` will be assigned the value 10.

Switch Statement

The `switch` statement is similar to an `if` statement except that it does not work with a range of values. A `switch` statement requires each case to be based on a single value. Depending on the value of the variable used for switching, the program will execute the correct block of code.

The syntax of a `switch` statement is as follows:

```
switch (variable used for switching)
{
    case firstCase:
        do A;
        break (or other jump statements);

    case secondCase:
        do B;
        break (or other jump statements);

    case default:
        do C;
        break (or other jump statements);
}
```

You can have as many cases as you want when using a `switch` statement. The `default` case is optional and is executed if no other case applies.

When a certain case is satisfied, everything starting from the next line is executed until a jump statement is reached. A jump statement is a statement that instructs the compiler to jump to another line in the program. We'll look at jump statements in greater depth later. The most commonly used jump statement is the `break;` statement.

Let's look at an example of how the `switch` statement works.

```
1 Console.Write("Enter your grade: ");
2 string userGrade = Console.ReadLine();
3
4 switch (userGrade)
5 {
6   case "A+":
7   case "A":
8       Console.WriteLine("Distinction");
9       break;
10  case "B":
11      Console.WriteLine("B Grade");
12      break;
13  case "C":
```

```
14       Console.WriteLine("C Grade");
15       break;
16    default:
17       Console.WriteLine("Fail");
18       break;
19 }
```

The program first prompts the user for his grade.

If grade is "A+" (Line 6), the program executes the next statement until it reaches the `break;` statement. This means it'll execute Line 7 to 9. Thus the output is "Distinction".

If grade is "A" (Line 7), the program executes Line 8 and 9. Similarly, the output is "Distinction".

If grade is not "A+" or "A", the program checks the next case. It keeps checking from top to bottom until a case is satisfied. If none of the cases applies, the default case is executed.

If you run the code above, you'll get the following output for each of the input shown:

```
Enter your grade: A+
Distinction

Enter your grade: A
Distinction

Enter your grade: B
B Grade

Enter your grade: C
C Grade

Enter your grade: D
Fail

Enter your grade: Hello
Fail
```

For Loop

The `for` loop executes a block of code repeatedly until the test condition is no longer valid.

The syntax for a `for` loop is as follows:

```
for (initial value; test condition; modification to
value)
{
    //Do Some Task
}
```

To understand how the `for` loop works, let's consider the example below.

```
1 for (int i = 0; i < 5; i++)
2 {
3    Console.WriteLine(i);
4 }
```

The main focus of the `for` loop is Line 1:

```
for (int i = 0; i < 5; i++)
```

There are three parts to it, each separated by a semi-colon.

The first part declares and initializes an `int` variable i to zero. This variable serves as a loop counter.

The second part tests if i is smaller than 5. If it is, the statements inside the curly braces will be executed. In this example, the curly braces are optional as there is only one statement.

After executing the `WriteLine()` statement, the program returns to the last segment in Line 1. `i++` increments the value of i by 1. Hence, i is increased from 0 to 1.

After the increment, the program tests if the new value of i is still smaller than 5. If it is, it executes the `WriteLine()` statement once again. This process of testing and incrementing the loop counter is repeated until the condition i < 5 is no longer true. At this point, the program exits the `for` loop and continues to execute other commands after the `for` loop.

The output for the code segment is:

```
0
1
2
3
4
```

The output stops at 4 because when i is 5, the `WriteLine()` statement is not executed as 5 is not smaller than 5.

The `for` loop is commonly used to loop through an array or a list. For instance, if we have

```
int[] myNumbers = { 10, 20, 30, 40, 50 };
```

we can use a `for` loop and the `Length` property of the array to loop through the array as shown below.

```
for (int i = 0; i < myNumbers.Length; i++)
{
    Console.WriteLine(myNumbers[i]);
}
```

As `myNumbers.Length` is equal to 5, this code runs from i = 0 to i = 4. If we run the code, we'll get the following output:

```
10
20
30
40
50
```

Foreach Loop

In addition to `for` loops, we can also use a `foreach` loop when working with arrays and lists. A `foreach` loop is very useful if you want to get information from an array or list, without making any changes to it.

Suppose you have

```
char[] message = { 'H', 'e', 'l', 'l', 'o' };
```

You can use the following code to display the elements of the array.

```
foreach (char i in message)
    Console.Write(i);
```

In the code above, we have a `char` variable i that is used for looping. Each time the loop runs, an element in the `message` array is assigned to the variable i. For instance, the first time the loop runs, the character 'H' is assigned to i.

The line

```
Console.Write(i);
```

then prints out the letter 'H'.

The second time the loop runs, the character 'e' is assigned to i. The line

```
Console.Write(i);
```

prints out the letter 'e'.

This continues until all the elements in the array have been printed.

While Loop

Like the name suggests, a `while` loop repeatedly executes instructions inside the loop while a certain condition remains valid. The structure of a `while` statement is as follows:

```
while (condition is true)
{
    do A
}
```

Most of the time when using a `while` loop, we need to first declare a variable to function as a loop counter. Let's call this variable `counter`. The code below shows an example of how a `while` loop works.

```
int counter = 5;

while (counter > 0)
{
    Console.WriteLine("Counter = {0}", counter);
    counter = counter - 1;
}
```

If you run the code, you'll get the following output

```
Counter = 5
Counter = 4
Counter = 3
Counter = 2
Counter = 1
```

A `while` statement has a relatively simple syntax. The statements inside the curly braces are executed as long as `counter > 0`.

Notice that we have the line `counter = counter - 1` inside the curly braces? This line is crucial. It decreases the value of `counter` by 1 each time the loop is run.

We need to decrease the value of `counter` by 1 so that the loop condition (`counter > 0`) will eventually evaluate to `false`. If we forget to do that, the loop will keep running endlessly, resulting in an infinite loop. The program will keep printing `counter = 5` until you somehow kill the program. Not a pleasant experience especially if you have a large program and you have no idea which code segment is causing the infinite loop.

Do while

The `do while` loop is similar to the `while` loop with one main difference - the code within the curly braces of a `do while` loop is executed at least once. Here's an example of how a `do while` loop works.

```
int counter = 100;

do {
    Console.WriteLine("Counter = {0}", counter);
    counter++;
} while (counter<0);
```

As the test condition (`while (counter<0)`) is placed after the closing curly brace, it is tested after the code inside the curly braces is executed at least once.

If you run the code above, you will get

```
Counter = 100;
```

After the `WriteLine()` statement is executed for the first time, `counter` is incremented by 1. The value of `counter` is now 101. When the program reaches the test condition, the test fails as `counter` is not smaller than 0. The program will then exit the loop. Even though the original value of `counter` does not meet the test condition (`counter < 0`), the code inside the curly braces is still executed once.

Note that for a `do while` statement, a semi-colon (`;`) is required after the test condition.

Jump Statements

We've now covered most of the control flow statements in C#. Next, let us look at jump statements.

A jump statement is a statement that instructs the program to deviate from its normal flow sequence and jump to another line of code. Jump statements are commonly used in loops and other control flow statements.

Break

The break keyword causes the program to exit a loop prematurely when a certain condition is met. We have already seen how the break keyword can be used in a switch statement. Now, let us look at an example of how the break keyword can be used in a for loop.

Consider the code segment below:

```
1 int i = 0;
2
3 for (i = 0; i < 5; i++)
4 {
5    Console.WriteLine("i = {0}", i);
6    if (i == 2)
7        break;
8 }
```

In this example, we used an if statement inside a for loop. It is very common for us to 'mix-and-match' various control tools in programming, such as using a while loop inside an if statement or using a for loop inside a while loop. This is known as a nested control statement.

If you run the code segment above, you will get the following output.

```
i =  0
i =  1
i =  2
```

Notice that the loop ends prematurely at $i = 2$?

Without the break keyword, the loop should run from $i = 0$ to $i = 4$ because the loop condition is $i < 5$. However with the break keyword, when $i = 2$, the condition on line 6 evaluates to true. The break keyword on line 7 then causes the loop to end prematurely.

Continue

Another commonly used jump keyword is the continue keyword. When we use continue, the rest of the loop after the keyword is skipped for that iteration. An example will make it clearer.

If you run the code segment below

```
for (int i = 0; i<5; i++)
{
    Console.WriteLine("i = {0}", i);
    if (i == 2)
      continue;
    Console.WriteLine("I will not be printed if
i=2.\n");
}
```

You will get the following output:

```
i =  0
I will not be printed if i=2.

i =  1
I will not be printed if i=2.

i =  2
i =  3
I will not be printed if i=2.

i =  4
I will not be printed if i=2.
```

When `i = 2`, the line after the `continue` keyword is not executed. Other than that, everything runs as per normal.

Exception Handling

We've now learned how to control the flow of a program under 'normal' circumstances using control flow statements and jump statements. Before we end this chapter, we need to look at one last control statement, the `try-catch-finally` statement. The `try-catch-finally` statement controls how the program proceeds when an error occurs. The syntax is as follows:

```
try
{
    do something
}
catch (type of error)
{
    do something else when an error occurs
}
finally
{
    do this regardless of whether the try or catch
condition is met.
}
```

You can have more than one `catch` blocks. In addition, the `finally` block is optional.

Let's consider an example.

```
int numerator, denominator;

Console.Write("Please enter the numerator: ");
numerator = Convert.ToInt32(Console.ReadLine());

Console.Write("Please enter the denominator: ");
denominator = Convert.ToInt32(Console.ReadLine());

try
```

```
{
    Console.WriteLine("The result is {0}.",
numerator/denominator);
}
catch (Exception e)
{
    Console.WriteLine(e.Message);
}
finally
{
    Console.WriteLine("---- End of Error Handling
Example ----");
}
```

If you run the code and enter 12 and 4, you'll get the message

```
The result is 3.
---- End of Error Handling Example ----
```

In this example, the code in the `try` block executes successfully. After the code in the `try` block is executed, the code in the `finally` block is executed.

Now suppose you enter 12 and 0 instead. You'll get

```
Attempted to divide by zero.
---- End of Error Handling Example ----
```

In this case, the code in the `catch` block is executed instead. This is because when the program tries to execute the statement in the `try` block, an error occurs since you cannot divide a number by zero. Hence, the statement in the `catch` block is executed. In addition, the code in the `finally` block is also executed. The `finally` block is always executed regardless of whether the `try` or `catch` block is executed.

The `catch` block allows us to specify the type of error that it should catch. In this case, we are trying to catch a general error. Therefore, we write

```
catch (Exception e)
```

where `Exception` refers to the class that the error belongs to and `e` is the name given to the error.

The `Exception` class handles all general errors and has a property called `Message` that explains the reason for the exception. To display that property, we write

```
Console.WriteLine(e.Message);
```

Specific Errors

In addition to the `Exception` class that handles general errors, we also have other classes that can handle more specific errors. This is useful if you want to perform specific tasks depending on the error caught. For instance, you may want to display your own error message.

Try running the code below:

```
int choice = 0;

int[] numbers = { 10, 11, 12, 13, 14, 15 };
Console.Write("Please enter the index of the array: ");

try
{
    choice = Convert.ToInt32(Console.ReadLine());
    Console.WriteLine("numbers[{0}] = {1}", choice,
numbers[choice]);
}catch (IndexOutOfRangeException)
{
    Console.WriteLine("Error: Index should be from 0
to 5.");
}catch (FormatException)
{
    Console.WriteLine("Error: You did not enter an
integer.");
}catch (Exception e)
{
    Console.WriteLine(e.Message);
```

```
}
```

If you enter

```
10
```

You will get

```
Index was outside the bounds of the array.
Index should be from 0 to 5.
```

If you enter

```
Hello
```

You will get

```
Input string was not in a correct format.
You did not enter an integer.
```

The first error is a `IndexOutOfRangeException` exception and was handled by the first `catch` block. This exception occurs when you try to access an element of an array with an index that is outside its bounds.

The second error is a `FormatException` exception and was handled by the second `catch` block. The `FormatException` exception occurs when the format of an argument is invalid. In our example, `Convert.ToInt32("Hello")` generated a `FormatException` exception as the argument "Hello" cannot be converted into an integer. In contrast, if you entered 4, `Convert.ToInt32("4")` will not generate a `FormatException` exception as the string "4" can be converted into an integer.

After the two specific `catch` blocks, we have one more `catch` block to catch any general errors that we did not pre-empt.

This example above shows two of the many exceptions in C#. For a complete list of all exceptions, refer to https://msdn.microsoft.com/en-us/library/system.systemexception.aspx.

Chapter 7: Object-Oriented Programming Part 1

We have covered a fair bit so far. In the next two chapters, we are going to look at another important concept in programming – the concept of object-oriented programming.

In this chapter, we'll learn what object-oriented programming is and how to write our own classes and create objects from them. In addition, we'll also discuss the concept of fields, properties, constructors and methods.

What is Object-Oriented Programming?

Simply stated, object-oriented programming is an approach to programming that breaks a programming problem into objects that interact with each other.

Objects are created from templates known as classes. You can think of a class as the blueprint of a building. An object is the actual "building" that we build based on the blueprint.

Writing our own class

To write our own class, we use the `class` keyword, following by the name of the class.

For instance, to create a `Staff` class, we write

```
class Staff {
    //Contents of the class
    //including fields, properties and methods
}
```

It is common practice to use PascalCasing when naming our classes. PascalCasing refers to the practice of capitalizing the first letter of each word, including the first word (e.g. `ThisIsAClassName`). This is the convention that we'll be following in the book.

The content of the class is enclosed within the pair of curly braces that follow the class name. Contents of a class include constructors, destructors, constants, fields, methods, properties, indexers, operators, events, delegates, interfaces, structs and other classes.

We'll cover some of the more common elements of a class in this chapter, namely fields, methods, properties and constructors.

To understand what these are, let's build a class from scratch.

First, create a new Console Application project in Visual Studio Community and name this project "ClassDemo ".

Study the code that is automatically generated for you. Notice that inside the `ClassDemo` namespace, VSC has already created a class called `Program` for you? Inside the `Program` class, we have the `Main()` method.

By default, the `Main()` method (which is the starting point for all C# applications) is put into the `Program` class created by VSC. If we want, we can change the name of the `Program` class to something else, but the `Main()` method must be called `Main()`. The `Main()` method must be present in all C# programs.

In this chapter, we are going to add a second class to the `ClassDemo` namespace. We'll call this new class `Staff` and add fields, properties and methods to the class. The complete code for this chapter can be downloaded at http://www.learncodingfast.com/csharp.

Let's first declare the class. Add the following code just before the line `class Program` in our auto-generated code.

```
class Staff
{
}
```

We now have two classes in our project: `Staff` and `Program`.

Fields

Inside the `Staff` class, add the following lines:

```
private string nameOfStaff;
private const int hourlyRate = 30;
private int hWorked;
```

Here, we declare one `string` variable (`nameOfStaff`) and two `int` variables (`hourlyRate` and `hWorked`). These variables are known as fields of the class. A field is simply a variable that is declared inside a class. Like any other variables, they are used to store data.

Notice that there is a word `private` in front of each declaration statement? This is known as an access modifier. Access modifiers are like gate keepers, they control who has access to that field (i.e. who can read and modify the value of that field).

A field can either be `private`, `public`, `protected` or `internal`. In our case, we declared the three fields as `private`. This means they can only be accessed from within the `Staff` class itself.

There are two reasons why we do not want the three fields to be accessible outside the class.

The first reason is that there is no need for other classes to know about those fields. In our case, the field `hourlyRate` is only needed within the `Staff` class. We have a method inside the `Staff` class that uses the field `hourlyRate` to calculate the monthly salary of an employee. Other classes do not use the `hourlyRate` field at all. Hence, it is appropriate to declare `hourlyRate` as `private` so as to hide this field from other classes.

This is known as encapsulation. Encapsulation enables an object to hide data and behaviour from other classes that do not need to know about them. This makes it easier for us to make changes to our code in future if necessary. We can safely change the value of `hourlyRate` inside `Staff` class without affecting other classes.

The second reason for declaring a field as `private` is that we do not want other classes to freely modify them. This helps to prevent the fields from being corrupted.

We'll talk more about access modifiers in the next chapter.

In addition to the `private` keyword, we also added the `const` keyword when we declared the `hourlyRate` field.

```
private const int hourlyRate = 30;
```

The `const` keyword indicates that the value cannot be changed after it is created. Any variable that is declared as `const` must be initialized at the point of declaration. In our example, we initialized `hourlyRate` to 30. This value cannot be changed subsequently anywhere in the code.

Properties

Next, let us look at properties.

A property is commonly used to provide access to a private field in cases where the field is needed by other classes. This may sound like a contradiction. Earlier, we mentioned that we use private fields so that other classes do not have access to them. If that is the case, why are we allowing access to them via properties?

One of the main reasons is that using properties gives us greater control over what rights other classes have when assessing these private fields. We'll see how to do that later.

For now, let us first learn how to declare a property.

Add the following lines of code to our `Staff` class, just after the line `private int hWorked;`.

```
public int HoursWorked
{
    get
    {
        return hWorked;
```

```
    }
    set
    {
        if (value > 0)
            hWorked = value;
        else
            hWorked = 0;
    }
}
```

We declared our property as

```
public int HoursWorked
{
}
```

The access modifier is `public` as we want other classes to have access to this property.

The data type is `int` because this property is used to provide access to the private `int` field `hWorked`. `hWorked` is known as the backing field of the property.

The name of the property is `HoursWorked`. We normally use PascalCasing for property names.

A property contains two special methods known as accessors. The first accessor is a getter and the second is a setter.

The basic getter simply returns the value of the private field. Hence, we write

```
get
{
    return hWorked;
}
```

where `return` is a keyword and `hWorked` is the name of the backing field.

The setter sets the value of the private field. We write

```
set
{
    if (value > 0)
        hWorked = value;
    else
        hWorked = 0;
}
```

value is a keyword when it used inside a setter. It refers to the value that is on the right side of the assignment statement when users use the property to set the value of the private field. We'll learn how to do that later.

Inside the setter, we did a simple check using an if statement. We checked if value is more than zero. If it is, we assign it to hWorked. Else, we set hWorked to zero. This setter demonstrates how we can use properties to control what values can be assigned to our private field.

By default, getter and setter have the same access level as the property itself (public in this case). Hence, we do not need to specify them. However, if you do not want the setter to have the same access level as the property, you can declare the setter as private so that other classes cannot modify your private field:

```
private set
{
}
```

The property is then a read-only property outside the Staff class. Its value can only be set within the Staff class itself.

Auto-implemented Properties

Note that in cases where no additional logic is required in the getter and setter, C# provides us with a shorthand to declare the property. This is known as an auto-implemented property.

To declare an auto-implemented property, we write

```
public int HoursWorked { get; set; }
```

This is equivalent to

```
private int hWorked;
public int HoursWorked
{
    get
    {
        return hWorked;
    }
    set
    {
        hWorked = value;
    }
}
```

When you use this shorthand, you do not have to declare a private field. The compiler will create an anonymous private backing field for you automatically.

If you want to make the property read-only, you can set the setter to `private` like this:

```
public int HoursWorked { get; private set; }
```

Methods

Next, let us look at methods.

A method is a code block that performs a certain task.

Let's add a simple method to our `Staff` class.

```
public void PrintMessage()
{
    Console.WriteLine("Calculating Pay…");
}
```

This method is declared as

```
public void PrintMessage()
{
}
```

The method declaration first states the accessibility level of the method. Here we declared the method as `public` so that the method is accessible everywhere in the program (not just within the `Staff` class).

Next, we state the return type of the method. A method may return a certain result after performing its task. If the method does not return any result, we use the `void` keyword like in our example.

Finally, we state the name of the method (`PrintMessage` in our example).

The parenthesis () after the method name is where we include the parameters of the method. Parameters are names given to data that we pass in to the method in order for it to perform its task. If the method requires no data (like in our example), we just add a pair of empty parenthesis after the method name.

After we declare the method, we define what it does inside the pair of curly braces that follow. This is known as implementing the method. In our example, the `PrintMessage()` method simply prints the line "Calculating Pay...".

That's all there is to the `PrintMessage()` method.

Next, let us move on to a more complex method. This second method calculates the pay of each employee and returns the result of the calculation. Add the following lines of code to `Staff`.

```
public int CalculatePay()
{
    PrintMessage();

    int staffPay;
    staffPay = hWorked * hourlyRate ;

    if (hWorked > 0)
```

```
        return staffPay;
    else
        return 0;
}
```

This method is declared as

```
public int CalculatePay()
{
}
```

The `int` keyword indicates that this method returns a value that is of `int` type.

Inside the curly braces, we have the statement

```
PrintMessage();
```

This is known as calling the `PrintMessage()` method. When the program reaches this statement, it will execute the `PrintMessage()` method first and print the line "Calculating Pay..." before executing the rest of the `CalculatePay()` method. This example demonstrates how you can call one method inside another method.

Next, we declare a local variable called `staffPay` and assign the product of the private fields `hourlyRate` and `hWorked` to it.

A method can access all the fields and properties that are declared inside the class. In addition, it can declare its own variables. These are known as local variables and only exist within the method. An example is the `staffPay` variable in our example.

After assigning the `staffPay` variable, we use an `if` statement to determine what result the method should return.

A method usually has at least one return statement. `return` is a keyword that is used to return an answer from the method. There can be more than one return statement in a method. However, once the method executes a return statement, the method will exit.

In our example, if `hWorked` is greater than zero, the program will execute the statement

```
return staffPay;
```

and exit the method. This return value can then be assigned to a variable. For instance, if `hWorked` is 10 and `hourlyRate` is 20, we can use the statement

```
int pay = CalculatePay();
```

to assign the result of `CalculatePay()` to the variable `pay`. The value of `pay` will then be 200.

On the other hand, if `hWorked` is less than or equal to zero, the program will execute the statement

```
return 0;
```

and exit the method. The value of `pay` will be 0.

Overloading

In C# (and most other languages), you can create two methods of the same name as long as they have different signatures. This is known as overloading. The signature of a method refers to the name of the method and the parameters that it has.

Add the following method below the previous `CalculatePay()` method.

```
public int CalculatePay(int bonus, int allowance)
{
    PrintMessage();
    if (hWorked > 0)
        return hWorked * hourlyRate + bonus +
    allowance;
    else
        return 0;
}
```

The signature of the first method is `CalculatePay()` while that of the second method is `CalculatePay(int bonus, int allowance)`.

This second method has two parameters - `bonus` and `allowance`. It calculates the pay of the employees by adding the values of these two parameters to the product of `hWorked` and `hourlyRate`. In this example, we did not use a local variable to store the result of `hWorked * hourlyRate + bonus + allowance`. We simply return the result of the computation directly. This is perfectly fine. We'll learn how to use this method later.

The ToString() method

Finally, before we move on to the next section, we need to write one more method – the `ToString()` method.

The `ToString()` method is a special method that returns a string that represents the current class. In C#, all classes come with a pre-defined `ToString()` method. However, it is customary (and expected of us) to override this method. Overriding a method simply means writing our own version of the method.

Typically, the `ToString()` method that we write displays the values of the fields and properties of the class. Add the following code to the `Staff` class:

```
public override string ToString()
{
    return "Name of Staff = " + nameOfStaff + ",
hourlyRate = " + hourlyRate + ", hWorked = " +
hWorked;
}
```

As you can see, the `ToString()` method returns a `string` type. The string that it returns contains information about the `Staff` class. The `override` keyword in the method declaration indicates that this method overrides the default method. We'll discuss more about the `override` keyword in the next chapter.

Constructors

Now, let us look at constructors.

A constructor is a special method that is used to 'construct' an object from the class template. It is the first method that is called whenever we create an object from our class. Constructors are commonly used to initialize the fields of the class.

A constructor always has the same name as the class (Staff in our case) and does not return any value. We do not need to use the void keyword when declaring a constructor.

Add the following lines to our Staff class.

```
public Staff(string name)
{
    nameOfStaff = name;
    Console.WriteLine("\n" + nameOfStaff);
    Console.WriteLine("--------------------------");
}
```

In this constructor, we first initialize the field nameOfStaff with the string that is passed in to the constructor (name). We then display the value of nameOfStaff on the screen and underline it with a series of dashes.

Like any other methods, we can have more than one constructor as long as the signature is different. We can add another constructor to our class.

```
public Staff(string firstName, string lastName)
{
    nameOfStaff = firstName + " " + lastName;
    Console.WriteLine("\n" + nameOfStaff);
    Console.WriteLine("--------------------------");
}
```

This constructor has two parameters - firstName and lastName. The first line concatenates the two strings and assigns the resulting string to `nameOfStaff`. The next two lines print `nameOfStaff` on the screen and underline it with a series of dashes.

Declaring a constructor is optional. If you do not declare your own constructor, C# creates one for you automatically. The default constructor simply initializes all the fields in the class to default values, which is normally zero for numeral fields and empty string for string fields.

Instantiating an Object

Now that we know how to create a class, let's look at how we can make use of the class to create an object. This process is known as instantiating an object. An object is also known as an instance.

To recap, our `Staff` class has the following components:

Fields

```
private const int hourlyRate
private string nameOfStaff
private int hWorked
```

Properties

```
public int HoursWorked
```

Methods

```
public void PrintMessage()
public int CalculatePay()
public int CalculatePay(int bonus, int allowance)
public override string ToString()
```

Constructors

```
public Staff(string name)
public Staff(string firstName, string lastName)
```

We shall instantiate a `Staff` object in the `Main()` method inside the `Program` class.

The syntax for instantiating an object is

```
ClassName objectName = new ClassName(arguments);
```

Add the following lines inside the curly braces of the `Main()` method in the `Program` class.

```
int pay;

Staff staff1 = new Staff("Peter");
staff1.HoursWorked = 160;
pay = staff1.CalculatePay(1000, 400);
Console.WriteLine("Pay = {0}", pay);
```

Here, we use the first constructor (with one parameter) to create our `staff1` object.

Once we create the object, we can use the dot operator after the object's name to access any public field, property or method in the `Staff` class. Note that we need to use the dot operator here as we are trying to access members of the `Staff` class from the `Program` class. The dot operator is necessary whenever we want to access a field, property or method from another class.

If you are accessing members of the same class, you do not need to use the dot operator. An example is when we called the `PrintMessage()` method from the `CalculatePay()` method earlier. We did not use the dot operator as both methods are from the same class.

After creating our `staff1` object, the next line shows how we can use the public `EmployeeType` property to assign a value to the `hWorked` field.

```
staff1.HoursWorked = 160;
```

If we try to access the private field `hWorked` directly by writing

```
staff1.hWorked = 160;
```

we will get an error as `hWorked` is a private field and is therefore only accessible within the `Staff` class.

To call the `CalculatePay()` method, we write

```
staff1.CalculatePay(1000, 400);
```

In this example, as we have the numbers 1000 and 400 inside the parenthesis, we are using the second `CalculatePay()` method. We are passing in the values 1000 and 400 to the parameters `bonus` and `allowance` respectively. The values that we passed in are known as arguments. The program then uses that method to calculate the pay and return the answer. This answer is assigned to the variable `pay`.

Finally, we use the `Console.WriteLine()` method to display the value of `pay` on the screen.

If you run the code above, you will get

```
Peter
-------------------------
Calculating Pay...
Pay = 6200
```

Play around with the code a bit to get a better feel of how classes work. Try adding the following lines of code

```
Staff staff2 = new Staff("Jane", "Lee");
staff2.HoursWorked = 160;
pay = staff2.CalculatePay();
Console.WriteLine("Pay = {0}", pay);
```

If you run the code above, you will get

```
Jane Lee
-------------------------
Calculating Pay...
Pay = 4800
```

Finally, let's create a third object to demonstrate how data validation works when we use properties. Add the following lines of code.

```
Staff staff3 = new Staff("Carol");
staff3.HoursWorked = -10;
pay = staff3.CalculatePay();
Console.WriteLine("Pay = {0}", pay);
```

Here, we tried to set the HoursWorked property to -10, which is an invalid value. The setter of that property sets the value to zero instead. If you run this code, you will get

```
Carol
--------------------------
Calculating Pay...
Pay = 0
```

Static Keyword

We've covered some pretty complicated concepts in this chapter. I strongly suggest that you download the complete program for this chapter from http://www.learncodingfast.com/csharp and play around with it. Study the code and make sure you fully understand the topics covered in this chapter so far before moving on.

In this section, we'll look at another keyword that is sometimes used when we declare classes or class members (i.e. methods, fields, properties, constructors etc).

Previously, we looked at how we can use the Staff class to create our staff1, staff2 and staff3 objects. However, there are some classes or class members that can be accessed without the need to create any objects. These are known as static classes or class members and are declared using the static keyword.

Consider the following class:

```
1 class MyClass
2 {
```

```
3    //Non static members
4    public string message = "Hello World";
5    public string Name { get; set; }
6    public void DisplayName()
7    {
8        Console.WriteLine("Name = {0}", Name);
9    }
10
11   //Static members
12   public static string greetings = "Good morning";
13   public static int Age { get; set; }
14   public static void DisplayAge()
15   {
16       Console.WriteLine("Age = {0}", Age);
17   }
18 }
```

MyClass contains one non static field `message`, one non static property `Name` and one non static method `DisplayName()` (lines 4 to 9).

It also contains one static field `greetings`, one static property `Age` and one static method `DisplayAge()` (lines 12 to 17).

To access the <u>non static</u> members of `MyClass` from another class, we need to instantiate an object as before:

```
MyClass classA = new MyClass();

Console.WriteLine(classA.message);
classA.Name = "Jamie";
classA.DisplayName();
```

However, to access the <u>static</u> members, we do not need to create any object. We simply use the class name to access them as shown below.

```
Console.WriteLine(MyClass.greetings);
MyClass.Age = 39;
MyClass.DisplayAge();
```

If you run the code above, you will get the following output

```
Hello World
Name = Jamie
Good Morning
Age = 39
```

In addition to having static methods, fields, properties and constructors, we can also have static classes. A static class can only contain static members. An example is shown below.

```
static class MyStaticClass
{
    public static int a = 0;
    public static int B{get; set;}
}
```

Some of the pre-written classes in C# are declared as static classes. An example is the `Console` class. We do not need to create a `Console` object when using methods from the `Console` class. We simply write `Console.WriteLine("Hello World");`.

Advanced Method Concepts

Now that you are familiar with classes, let us move on to some advanced concepts regarding the declaration and use of methods in a class. These concepts are more complex and may require more than one reading to fully understand them.

Using Arrays and Lists

Previously, we learned how to use basic data types like `int` and `float` as parameters to a method. In addition to using basic data types, we can also use arrays and lists.

To use an array as a parameter, we add a square bracket [] after the parameter's data type in the method declaration. An example is shown below.

```
public void PrintFirstElement(int[] a)
{
```

```
    Console.WriteLine("The first element is {0}.\n",
a[0]);
}
```

To call this method, we need to declare an array and pass it in as an argument to the method:

```
int[] myArray = {1, 2, 3, 4, 5};
PrintFirstElement(myArray);
```

The next example shows how we can use a list as a parameter.

```
public void PrintFirstListElement(List<int> a)
{
    Console.WriteLine("The first list element is
{0}.\n", a[0]);
}
```

To call the method, we need to declare a list and pass it in as an argument to the method.

```
List<int> myList = new List<int> {1, 2, 3};
PrintFirstListElement(myList);
```

In addition to using arrays or lists as parameters to a method, we can also return an array or list from a method. To return an array from a method, we add a square bracket [] after the return type in the method declaration.

```
public int[] ReturnUserInput()
{
    int[] a = new int[3];

    for (int i = 0; i < a.Length; i++)
    {
        Console.Write("Enter an integer: ");
        a[i] = Convert.ToInt32(Console.ReadLine());
        Console.WriteLine("Integer added to
    array.\n");
    }
```

```
    return a;
}
```

To use this method, we need to declare an array and assign the method's result to it.

```
int[] myArray2 = ReturnUserInput ();
```

To return a list from a method, we use the `List<>` keyword as the return type in the method declaration. An example is

```
public List<int> ReturnUserInputList()
{
    List<int> a = new List<int>();
    int input;

    for (int i = 0; i < 3; i++)
    {
        Console.Write("Enter an integer: ");
        input = Convert.ToInt32(Console.ReadLine());
        Console.WriteLine("Integer added to
    list.\n");
        a.Add(input);
    }
    return a;
}
```

To use this method, we need to declare a list and assign the method's result to it.

```
List<int> myList2 = ReturnUserInputList();
```

Using params keyword

Next, let's explore the `params` keyword. The `params` keyword is useful when we do not know the number of arguments a method has. For instance, we may have a method that prints a series of names, but we do not know how many names there are in advance. In cases like this, we can use an array as the parameter and add the `params` keyword in front of it.

An example is

```
public void PrintNames(params string[] names)
{
    for (int i = 0; i < names.Length; i++)
    {
        Console.Write(names[i] + " ");
    }
    Console.WriteLine();
}
```

To use this method, we can pass in any number of strings as arguments.

Example

```
PrintNames("Peter");
PrintNames("Yvonne", "Jamie");
PrintNames("Abigail", "Betty", "Carol", "David");
```

Output

```
Peter
Yvonne Jamie
Abigail Betty Carol David
```

Note that no additional parameters are permitted after the `params` keyword in a method declaration, and only one `params` keyword is permitted in a method declaration.

Hence, the following method declaration is fine

```
public void PrintNames2(int a, double b, params int[] ages)
```

but the following declarations are not

```
public void PrintNames3(int a, params string[] names, double b)
```

```
public void PrintNames4(params string[] names, params
int[] ages)
```

PrintNames3 is not allowed because double b comes after
params string[] names.

PrintNames4 is not allowed because there are two params keywords.

Passing Value Type vs Reference Type Parameters

I hope you now have a good understanding of how classes and methods
work. Before we end this chapter, I'd like to revisit the concept of value
data types and reference data types. In Chapter 4, we learnt that there
are two main categories of data types in C# - value types and reference
types. There is a difference when you pass in a value type variable to a
method vs a reference type variable.

When you pass in a value type variable, any change made to the value
of that variable is only valid within the method itself. Once the program
exits the method, the change is no longer valid.

On the other hand, if you pass in a reference type variable, any change
made to the variable is valid even after the method ends.

Consider the class below:

```
class MethodDemo
{
    public void PassByValue(int a)
    {
        a = 10;
        Console.WriteLine("a inside method = {0}",
    a);
    }

    public void PassByReference(int[] b)
    {
        b[0] = 5;
        Console.WriteLine("b[0] inside method = {0}",
    b[0]);
```

```
        }
}
```

Within the class, we have two methods. The first method accepts a value type variable and tries to change the value of that variable. It then prints the value of the variable.

The second method accepts an array (reference type) and tries to change the value of the first element in the array. It then prints the value of that element.

In our `Main()` program, suppose we have the following lines of code:

```
int a = 2;
int[] b = { 1, 2, 3 };
MethodDemo obj = new MethodDemo();

Console.WriteLine("a before = {0}", a);
obj.PassByValue(a);
Console.WriteLine("a after = {0}", a);

Console.WriteLine("\n\n");

Console.WriteLine("b[0] before = {0}", b[0]);
obj.PassByReference(b);
Console.WriteLine("b[0] after = {0}", b[0]);
```

If you run the program, you will get

```
a before = 2
a inside method = 10
a after = 2

b[0] before = 1
b[0] inside method = 5
b[0] after = 5
```

The value of a stays the same before and after the method call; the change is only valid inside the method itself.

On the other hand, the value of `b[0]` changes after the method call.

Be aware of this difference when you pass in a value type variable to a method (e.g. `int, float` etc) vs a reference type variable (such as an array or list).

Chapter 8: Object-Oriented Programming Part 2

Now, let us move on to some of the more advanced topics in object-oriented programming. In this chapter, we'll learn about inheritance, polymorphism, abstract classes and interfaces.

Inheritance

Inheritance is one of the key concepts of object-oriented programming. Simply stated, inheritance allows us to create a new class from an existing class so that we can effectively reuse existing code.

Writing the Parent Class

Suppose we are writing a program for a fitness club that has two types of membership – VIP and Normal. To do that, let's create a class called `Member` first.

```
class Member
{
    protected int annualFee;
    private string name;
    private int memberID;
    private int memberSince;
}
```

`Member` contains one protected field and three private fields. A protected field is a field that is only accessible within the class in which it is declared and any class that is derived from it. We'll talk about derived classes very soon.

Next, let us write a `ToString()` method to display the values of the four fields.

```
public override string ToString()
{
```

```
    return "\nName: " + name + "\nMember ID: " +
memberID + "\nMember Since: " + memberSince +
"\nTotal Annual Fee: " + annualFee;
}
```

Finally, let's add two constructors to the `Member` class.

```
public Member()
{
    Console.WriteLine("Parent Constructor with no
parameter");
}

public Member(string pName, int pMemberID, int
pMemberSince)
{
    Console.WriteLine("Parent Constructor with 3
parameters");

    name = pName;
    memberID = pMemberID;
    memberSince = pMemberSince;
}
```

The first constructor merely prints the line "Parent Constructor with no parameter".

The second constructor is more interesting. It prints the line "Parent Constructor with 3 parameters" and assigns its parameters to the three private fields in the `Member` class.

Writing the Child Class

Now, let us learn how to derive a class from the `Member` class. Derived classes are known as child classes, while the classes from which they are derived are known as parent classes or base classes.

A derived class inherits all the public and protected members from the parent class. In other words, it can use those fields, properties and methods as if they are part of its own code.

Our parent class (Member) has the following contents:

Fields

```
protected int annualFee
private string name
private int memberID
private int memberSince
```

Methods

```
public override string ToString()
```

Constructors

```
public Member()
public Member(string pName, int pMemberID, int
pMemberSince)
```

We shall derive two classes – NormalMember and VIPMember – from the Member class.

First, let's declare the child class NormalMember. We indicate that it is derived from the Member class using a colon (:) like this

```
class NormalMember : Member
{
}
```

Now, we need to write the constructor for the child class. The constructor of a child class is built upon the parent's constructor. Whenever we create a child object, the parent class constructor is always called first.

There are two ways to create a child constructor. The first way is to simply declare it like any other constructor.

```
public NormalMember()
{
    Console.WriteLine("Child constructor with no
parameter");
```

```
}
```

When we declare our constructor as above, C# looks for a parameterless constructor (i.e. a constructor with no parameter) in the parent class and calls that first before executing the code in the child constructor. If you use this constructor to create a child object, the following two lines will be displayed on the screen

```
Parent Constructor with no parameter
Child constructor with no parameter
```

The first line is from the parent constructor while the second line is from the child constructor.

The second way to declare a child constructor is to use the colon sign (:) and the base keyword to call a <u>non parameterless</u> constructor in the parent class. An example is shown below:

```
public NormalMember(string remarks) : base ("Jamie",
1, 2015)
{
    Console.WriteLine("Remarks = {0}", remarks);
}
```

When we call a non parameterless constructor in the parent class, we need to pass in values to its parameters. In the example above, we passed in the values "Jamie", 1 and 2015 to the parent constructor. These values are then assigned to the fields name, memberID and memberSince in the base class respectively.

In this example, we passed in fixed values as arguments to the base constructor. However, a better way is to pass in the arguments through the child constructor. The example below shows how this can be done. Replace the previous constructor with the constructor below:

```
public NormalMember(string remarks, string name, int
memberID, int memberSince) : base (name, memberID,
memberSince)
{
```

```
    Console.WriteLine("Child Constructor with 4
parameters");
    Console.WriteLine("Remarks = {0}", remarks);
}
```

This new child constructor has four parameters. The first parameter is a `string` parameter called `remarks`. This parameter is used inside the child constructor.

The second, third and fourth parameters are not used in the child constructor. Instead, they are passed in as arguments to the parent constructor based on their names. For instance, the second parameter in the child constructor (`string name`) is passed in as the first argument to the parent constructor (`name`).

When we create a child object with this constructor, we write something like

```
NormalMember myChildMember = new
NormalMember("Special Rate", "James", 1, 2010);
```

The base constructor with 3 parameters is called and executed first. The values "James", 1 and 2010 are passed to the base constructor. Behind the scene, these values are assigned to the fields `name`, `memberID` and `memberSince` in the base class respectively.

After executing the base constructor, the child constructor will be executed. The string "Special Rate" is assigned to `remarks` and displayed on the screen.

When you run the code, you will get the following output

```
Parent Constructor with 3 parameters
Child Constructor with 4 parameters
Remarks = Special Rate
```

Now that we have created the constructors for our child class, let us move on to create a method to calculate the annual fee of a normal member. The code is simply

```
public void CalculateAnnualFee()
{
    annualFee = 100 + 12*30;
}
```

When we write "annualFee" in the code above, we are accessing the protected field `annualFee` in the parent class. Recall that a child class has access to all public and protected fields in its parent class? Hence, the child class can use this field as if it is its own field. The child class does not need to create an instance of the parent class in order to access its protected fields.

That's all for our child class `NormalMember`. The class has the following contents:

Fields

Inherited from parent class:
```
protected int annualFee
```

Methods

Inherited from parent class:
```
public override string ToString()
```

Declared in child class:
```
public void CalculateAnnualFee()
```

Constructors

```
public NormalMember()
public NormalMember(string remarks, string name, int
memberID, int memberSince)
```

Next, let us write another class that inherits from `Member`. This time, the derived class is called `VIPMember`. The code is shown below.

```
class VIPMember : Member
{
```

```
    public VIPMember(string name, int memberID, int
memberSince) : base (name, memberID, memberSince)
    {
        Console.WriteLine("Child Constructor with 3
    parameters");
    }

    public void CalculateAnnualFee()
    {
        annualFee = 1200;
    }
}
```

This class has one constructor (with 3 parameters) and one method
CalculateAnnualFee(). The CalculateAnnualFee() method
here uses a different formula for calculating annual fee from the
CalculateAnnualFee() method in the NormalMember class. It is
alright for the two methods to share the same name (and signature) as
they are in different classes.

VIPMember class has the following contents:

Fields

Inherited from parent class:
protected int annualFee

Methods

Inherited from parent class:
public override string ToString()

Declared in child class:
public void CalculateAnnualFee()

Constructors

public VIPMember(string name, int memberID, int
memberSince)

The Main() method

Now that we have written the three classes that we need, let's write the code for the `Main()` method.

First, we'll create two objects from the two derived classes.

```
NormalMember mem1 = new NormalMember("Special Rate",
"James", 1, 2010);
VIPMember mem2 = new VIPMember("Andy", 2, 2011);
```

`mem1` is created using the 4 parameters constructor from the `NormalMember` class.
`mem2` is created using the 3 parameters constructor from the `VIPMember` class.

Next, we'll use the `CalculateAnnualFee()` methods in the respective classes.

```
mem1.CalculateAnnualFee();
mem2.CalculateAnnualFee();
```

As `mem1` is an instance of the `NormalMember` class, the `CalculateAnnualFee()` method from that class is executed. The annual fee for `mem1` is thus 100 + 12*30 = 460. For `mem2`, the annual fee is 1200 as it uses the method from the `VIPMember` class.

Finally, let's use the `ToString()` method from the parent class (`Member`) to display the information on our screen. We write

```
Console.WriteLine(mem1.ToString());
Console.WriteLine(mem2.ToString());
```

Since the `ToString()` method belongs to the parent class and is public, both `mem1` and `mem2` have inherited the method and are thus able to use it in the `Main()` method. This facilitates code reuse as we do not need to rewrite the `ToString()` method for both the child classes.

You'll get the following output when you run the program:

```
Parent Constructor with 3 parameters
Child Constructor with 4 parameters
Message = Special Rate
Parent Constructor with 3 parameters
Child Constructor with 3 parameters

Name: James
Member ID: 1
Member Since: 2010
Total Annual Fee: 460

Name: Andy
Member ID: 2
Member Since: 2011
Total Annual Fee: 1200
```

Polymorphism

Now that we have seen an example of how inheritance woks, let us move on to discuss another topic that is closely related to inheritance - the concept of polymorphism. Polymorphism refers to a program's ability to use the correct method for an object based on its run-time type.

The best way to explain polymorphism is through an example. Let's expand on our Fitness club example above.

First, delete all the code in the previous `Main()` method and add the following lines:

```
Member[] clubMembers = new Member[5];

clubMembers[0] = new NormalMember("Special Rate",
"James", 1, 2010);
clubMembers[1] = new NormalMember("Normal Rate",
"Andy", 2, 2011);
clubMembers[2] = new NormalMember("Normal Rate",
"Bill", 3, 2011);
clubMembers[3] = new VIPMember("Carol", 4, 2012);
clubMembers[4] = new VIPMember("Evelyn", 5, 2012);
```

Here, we declare an array of Member type and add 5 members to it. The first three members are instances of the NormalMember class while the last two are instances of the VIPMember class.

Although clubMembers is declared to be an array of Member type, we can assign instances of NormalMember and VIPMember to it as they are child classes of the Member class. We do not need to declare separate arrays for NormalMember and VIPMember objects.

Next, we'll use a foreach loop to calculate the annual fee of each member and display the information.

To do that, we write

```
foreach (Member m in clubMembers)
{
    m.CalculateAnnualFee();
    Console.WriteLine(m.ToString());
}
```

If you try to run the program at this stage, you'll get an error that says Member does not contain a definition for 'CalculateAnnualFee'. This is because clubMembers is declared to be an array of Member type. Hence, the complier tries to execute the CalculateAnnualFee() method in the Member class when we write m.CalculateAnnualFee(). An error occurs because we do not have such a method in our Member parent class; we only have it in the two child classes. To rectify this error, we have to add the following method to our parent class.

```
public void CalculateAnnualFee()
{
    annualFee = 0;
}
```

Now run the program and pay attention to the "Total Annual Fee" for each member. What do you notice? It should all show $0. This means the CalculateAnnualFee() method that is invoked is the one in the parent class. This is not surprising as `clubMembers` is declared to be of `Member` type.

If you want the child method to be invoked instead, you have to make two changes.

First, you need to declare the parent method as virtual, like this

```
public virtual void CalculateAnnualFee()
{
    annualFee = 0;
}
```

The `virtual` keyword tells the compiler that this method may be overridden in derived classes. When the compiler encounters this keyword, it'll look for the same method in the derived class and execute that method instead.

Next, in the derived class, you have to declare that your method overrides the method in the parent class using the `override` keyword, like this

```
//In VIPMember child class
public override void CalculateAnnualFee()
{
    annualFee = 1200;
}
```

```
//In NormalMember child class
public override void CalculateAnnualFee()
{
    annualFee = 100 + 12 * 30;
}
```

Now if you run the program again, the annual fee for the first three members (`NormalMember`) and the last two members (`VIPMember`) will be $460 and $1200 respectively.

This is the result of polymorphism. At run time (i.e. when the program runs), the program determines that the first three members of `clubMembers` are of `NormalMember` type and executes the `CalculateAnnualFee()` method from that class. It also determines that the last two members are of `VIPMember` type and executes the method from that class.

Polymorphism simply means that at run time, the program is smart enough to use the `CalculateAnnualFee()` method from the correct child class even when that object is declared to be of `Member` type.

We say that the runtime type of the first three elements of `clubMembers` is `NormalMember` while the runtime type of the last two elements is `VIPMember`. The declared type of all the 5 elements is `Member`.

GetType() and typeof()

In the previous example, we let the program determine the run time type of each member of the `clubMembers` array and invoke the correct `CalculateAnnualFee()` method. However, sometimes, it may be necessary for us to determine the runtime type of each individual member ourselves when we code. We'll see an example of that later in our project.

The `if` statement below shows how you can determine whether the first element of the `clubMember` array is of `VIPMember` type at run time:

```
if (clubMembers[0].GetType() == typeof(VIPMember))
    Console.WriteLine("Yes");
else
    Console.WriteLine("No");
```

The `GetType()` method returns the runtime type of an object.

The `typeof()` method takes the name of a data type (e.g. `int`, `float`, or the name of a class) and returns the type of that name, which we can then compare with the result of the `GetType()` method on the left.

If you run the code above, you'll get "No" as the output since `clubMembers[0]` is not of `VIPMember` type.

Abstract Classes and Methods

Now that we are familiar with inheritance (and polymorphism), let us move on to discuss two special types of "parent class" in C# - abstract classes and interfaces.

First, let's look at abstract classes.

An abstract class is a special type of class that is created strictly to be a base class for other classes to derive from. They cannot be instantiated. In other words, if `FourWheelVehicles` is an abstract class, the statement

```
FourWheelVehicle myVeh = new FourWheelVehicle();
```

will give you an error as you cannot create an object of an abstract class.

Abstract classes may have fields, properties and methods just like any other classes. However, they cannot have static members. In addition, abstract classes can have a special type of method known as abstract methods. Abstract methods are methods that have no body and MUST be implemented in the derived class. They can only exist in abstract classes. In a way, an abstract method is like a contract. If you want to ensure that any class that inherits your class implements a certain method, you can declare the class as an abstract class and the method as an abstract method.

To declare an abstract class, simply add the `abstract` keyword before the keyword `class` like this:

```
abstract class MyClass
{
}
```

To declare an abstract method inside an abstract class, add the `abstract` keyword before the return type, like this:

```
public abstract void MyAbstractMethod();
```

As abstract methods have no body, we end the declaration with a semi-colon (;).

To implement an abstract method in the derived class, we use the `override` keyword, like this.

```
public override void MyAbstractMethod()
{
}
```

The code below shows an example of an abstract class.

```
1 using System;
2 using System.Collections.Generic;
3 using System.Linq;
4 using System.Text;
5 using System.Threading.Tasks;
6
7 namespace AbstractClassDemo
8 {
9    class Program
10   {
11       static void Main(string[] args)
12       {
13           //MyAbstractClass abClass = new
MyAbstractClass();
14           ClassA a = new ClassA();
15           a.PrintMessage();
16           a.PrintMessageAbstract();
17           Console.Read();
18       }
19   }
20
21   abstract class MyAbstractClass
22   {
23       private string message = "Hello C#";
24       public void PrintMessage()
25       {
26           Console.WriteLine(message);
27       }
```

```
28        public abstract void PrintMessageAbstract();
29  }
30
31  class ClassA : MyAbstractClass
32  {
33        public override void PrintMessageAbstract()
34        {
35              Console.WriteLine("C# is fun!");
36        }
37  }
38 }
```

The abstract class is from Line 21 to 29. It contains a private field `message` and a public method `PrintMessage()`. It also contains an abstract method `PrintMessageAbstract()` on line 28. Lines 31 to 37 show the derived class which implements the abstract method (lines 33 to 36).

If you run the program above, you will get

```
Hello C#
C# is fun!
```

Notice that Line 13 is commented out with the // sign? If you remove the two slashes, you will get an error as an abstract class cannot be instantiated.

Interfaces

Next, let's look at interfaces. Interfaces are much like abstract classes in that they cannot be instantiated and must be inherited. However, interfaces are more conceptual than abstract classes. They can only contain methods with no bodies. In addition, they cannot contain fields but can contain properties. Interfaces also cannot have static members. When a child class inherits an interface, we say that it implements the interface.

One of the key differences between an abstract class and an interface is that a class can only inherit one abstract class but can implement multiple interfaces. We won't be showing an example of multiple interfaces implementation as that is an advanced topic beyond the scope of this book.

The code below shows an example of how a class can implement one interface. It is common to start the name of an interface with the letter I. All properties and methods in an interface are public, so there is no need to add any access modifiers to them.

```
1 using System;
2 using System.Collections.Generic;
3 using System.Linq;
4 using System.Text;
5 using System.Threading.Tasks;
6
7 namespace InterfaceDemo
8 {
9   class Program
10  {
11      static void Main(string[] args)
12      {
13          ClassA a = new ClassA();
14          a.MyNumber = 5;
15          a.InterfaceMethod();
16          Console.Read();
17      }
18  }
19
20  interface IShape
21  {
22      int MyNumber
23      {
24          get;
25          set;
26      }
27      void InterfaceMethod();
28  }
29
30  class ClassA : IShape
31  {
```

```
32
33        private int myNumber;
34        public int MyNumber
35        {
36            get
37            {
38                return myNumber;
39            }
40            set
41            {
42                if (value < 0)
43                    myNumber = 0;
44                else
45                    myNumber = value;
46            }
47        }
48
49        public void InterfaceMethod()
50        {
51            Console.WriteLine("The number is {0}.",
MyNumber);
52        }
53  }
54  }
```

The interface is declared on lines 20 to 28. On lines 22 to 26, we declared a property and on line 27, we declared a method.

ClassA implements the IShape interface. The property is implemented on lines 33 to 47 where we declared a private backing field (myNumber) for the property and implemented some control rules.

The method is implemented on lines 49 to 52. We do not need to use the override keyword when implementing a method that belongs to an interface.

If you run this program, you'll get

```
The number is 5.
```

Access Modifiers Revisited

Now that we have covered various topics related to inheritance, let us take a second look at the concept of access modifiers in object oriented programming. Earlier, we learnt that an access modifier is like a gate-keeper. It controls who has access to a certain field, property or method. C# comes with 4 access modifiers: `private`, `public`, `protected` and `internal`.

Anything declared as `internal` is only accessible within the current assembly. As we won't be covering assemblies in this book, we will not be demonstrating how `internal` works.

To understand how `private`, `public` and `protected` work, let's consider the example below. We'll be using fields to demonstrate the concept. The same applies to methods and properties.

Suppose we have a class with three fields:

```
class ClassA
{
    private int privateNum = 1;
    public int publicNum = 2;
    protected int protectedNum = 3;

}
```

If `ClassB` is derived from `ClassA`,

```
class ClassB:ClassA
{
    public void PrintMessages()
    {
        //This is ok
        Console.WriteLine(publicNum);

        //This is ok
        Console.WriteLine(protectedNum);
```

```
        //This is NOT ok
        Console.WriteLine(privateNum);
    }
}
```

the first two `WriteLine()` statements will not give us any error as a
derived class can access any public and protected fields in the parent
class.

However, the third statement gives us an error as `privateNum` is a
private field and is thus only accessible in `ClassA` itself.

If a class is <u>not derived</u> from `ClassA`, we need to instantiate a `ClassA`
object in order to access the public field of `ClassA`. However, even with
a `ClassA` object, we cannot access the private and protected fields of
`ClassA`. In the example below, `ClassC` is not derived from `ClassA`.
Hence, the first `WriteLine()` statement will not give us any error but
the second and third statements will.

```
class ClassC
{
    ClassA a = new ClassA();

    public void PrintMessages()
    {
        //This is ok
        Console.WriteLine(a.publicNum);

        //This is NOT ok
        Console.WriteLine(a.protectedNum);

         //This is NOT ok
        Console.WriteLine(a.privateNum);
    }
}
```

In short, anything that is declared as `public` is accessible everywhere;
there are no restrictions on accessing public members. On the other
hand, anything declared as `private` is only accessible within the class

in which it is declared. Anything declared as protected is accessible within the class in which it is declared and any class that is derived from it.

Chapter 9: Enum and Struct

In Chapter 3 and 4, we looked at some built in data types provided by C#. These include value types like `int`, `float` and `double` and reference data types like arrays, strings and lists. In addition, we also looked at how you can write your own classes in Chapter 7 and 8. A class can be considered to be an advanced user-defined data type that groups a set of related fields, properties and methods into a logical unit.

In this chapter, we are going to look at two more user-defined data types in C# – enum and struct.

Enum

An enum (which stands for enumerated type) is a special data type that allows programmers to provide meaningful names for a set of integral constants.

To declare an enum, we use the `enum` keyword followed by the name of the enum. The members of the enum are enclosed in a set of curly braces and separated by commas.

An example is shown below:

```
enum DaysOfWeek
{
    Sun, Mon, Tues, Wed, Thurs, Fri, Sat
}
```

Note that we <u>do not</u> put a semi-colon at the end of the last member.

After declaring the `DaysOfWeek` enum, we can declare and initialize a `DaysOfWeek` variable like this:

```
DaysOfWeek myDays = DaysOfWeek.Mon;
```

The name of the variable is `myDays`. If we write

```
Console.WriteLine(myDays);
```

we'll get

```
Mon
```

By default, each member in the enum is assigned an integer value, starting from zero. That is, in our example, Sun is assigned a value of 0, Mon is 1, Tues is 2 and so on.

As members of an enum are essentially integers, we can cast a `DaysOfWeek` variable into an `int` and vice versa. For instance,

```
Console.WriteLine((int)myDays);
```

gives us the integer `1` while

```
Console.WriteLine((DaysOfWeek)1);
```

gives us `Mon`.

If you want to assign a different set of integers to your enum members, you can do the following

```
enum DaysOfWeekTwo
{
    Sun = 5, Mon = 10, Tues, Wed, Thurs, Fri, Sat
}
```

Now, Sun is assigned a value of 5 and Mon is assigned 10. As we did not assign values for Tues to Sat, consecutive numbers after 10 will be assigned to them. That is Tues = 11, Wed = 12 and so on.

All enums are stored internally as integers (`int`). If you want to change the underlying data type from `int` to another data type, you add a colon after the enum name, followed by the desired data type. Any integer data type is allowed except for `char`. An example is

```
enum DaysOfWeekThree : byte
{
```

```
    Sun, Mon, Tues, Wed, Thurs, Fri, Sat
}
```

Of course, if you use a `byte` data type, you cannot do something like

```
enum DaysOfWeekFour : byte
{
    Sun = 300, Mon, Tues, Wed, Thurs, Fri, Sat
}
```

as the range for `byte` is from 0 to 255.

There are two main reasons for using enums. The first is to improve the readability of your code. The statement

```
myDays = DaysOfWeek.Mon;
```

is more self-explanatory than the statement

```
myDays = 1;
```

The second reason is to restrict the values that a variable can take. If we have a variable that stores the days of a week, we may accidentally assign the value 10 to it. This can be prevented when we use an enum as we can only assign the pre-defined members of the enum to the variable.

Struct

Now, let's look at the `struct` data type.

A struct is similar to a class in many aspects. Like classes, they contain elements like properties, constructors, methods and fields and allow you to group related members into a single package so that you can manipulate them as a group.

To declare a struct, you use the `struct` keyword. An example is:

```
1 struct MyStruct
2 {
3   //Fields
4   private int x, y;
5   private AnotherClass myClass;
6   private Days myDays;
7
8   //Constructor
9   public MyStruct(int a, int b, int c)
10  {
11      myClass = new AnotherClass();
12      myClass.number = a;
13      x = b;
14      y = c;
15      myDays = Days.Mon;
16  }
17
18  //Method
19  public void PrintStatement()
20  {
21      Console.WriteLine("x = {0}, y = {1}, myDays =
{2}", x, y, myDays);
22  }
23 }
24
25 class AnotherClass
26 {
27   public int number;
28 }
29
30 enum Days { Mon, Tues, Wed }
```

The struct is declared from lines 1 to 23. On line 4, we declared two
private int fields for the struct. On line 5, we declared another private
field called myClass. This field is an instance of the class
AnotherClass. On line 6, we declared an enum variable myDays. The
two fields (myClass and myDays) are specially included in this example
to demonstrate how we can include a class instance and an enum
variable as the fields of a struct. Structs (and classes) can contain enum
variables and instances of other structs and classes as fields.

After declaring the fields, we declared the constructor for the struct (lines 9 to 16), followed by a method to print the values of x, y and myDays. (lines 19 to 22).

After declaring the struct, we declared the class AnotherClass on lines 25 to 28 and the enum Days on line 30. In this example, we declared the class and enum outside the struct myStruct. However, it is possible for us to declare the enum or class inside the struct itself. An enum, struct or class can be nested inside another struct or class. We'll look at an example of an enum declared inside a class when we work through the project at the end of the book.

To use the struct above, we can add the following code to our Main() method:

```
MyStruct example = new MyStruct(2, 3, 5);
example.PrintStatement();
```

If we run the code, we'll get

```
x = 3, y = 5, myDays = Mon
```

There are two main differences between a struct and a class. Firstly, the struct data type does not support inheritance. Hence you cannot derive one struct from another. However, a struct can implement an interface. The way to do it is identical to how it is done with classes. Refer to Chapter 8 for more information.

The second difference between structs and classes is that structs are value types while classes are reference types.

For a complete list of differences between a struct and a class, check out the following page: https://msdn.microsoft.com/en-us/library/saxz13w4.aspx

Chapter 10: LINQ

LINQ stands for Language-Integrated Query and is an interesting feature of C# that allows you to query data in your program. In this chapter, we'll cover a brief introduction to LINQ followed by two examples of how LINQ can be used.

Let's first learn how to write a LINQ query. The typical syntax for a LINQ query is

```
from... where... orderby... select
```

Let's suppose we have an array of numbers and we want to select all even numbers from the array. We can do that easily with LINQ.

First, let's declare the array.

```
int[] numbers = { 0, 1, 2, 3, 4, 5, 6 };
```

Next, we write a LINQ query as follows:

```
var evenNumQuery =
    from num in numbers
    where (num % 2) == 0
    select num;
```

The query is from the second to the fourth line. Readers who have experience with SQL will probably find this query quite familiar. The query consists of three parts. The first part

```
from num in numbers
```

states that we are performing the query on the `numbers` array. `num` is the name that we use to represent the individual items in the array. The next line

```
where (num % 2) == 0
```

tests the individual items to determine if the remainder of `num` divided by 2 is zero. If it is, `num` is an even number. The third line

```
select num;
```

selects all elements that satisfy this criteria.

This result is then assigned to the variable `evenNumQuery`, which is declared to be of `var` type. `var` is a special data type that we use whenever we want the complier to determine the data type itself. This is necessary because in our example, the data type of `evenNumQuery` is quite complex; we are better off letting C# figure the data type out for us.

After we create the query statement, we can execute the query by writing

```
foreach (int i in evenNumQuery)
{
    Console.WriteLine("{0} is an even number", i);
}
```

If you run this code, you will get

```
0 is an even number
2 is an even number
4 is an even number
6 is an even number
```

That's it. That's how easy it is to use LINQ. Let us now move on to a more complex example of LINQ.

Suppose you have a `Customer` class with `Name`, `Phone`, `Address` and `Balance` as its properties and a constructor to initialize each of these properties.

We can create a list of `Customer` objects in our `Main()` method using the code below.

```
List<Customer> customers = new List<Customer>();
```

```
customers.Add(new Customer("Alan", "80911291", "ABC
Street", 25.60m));
customers.Add(new Customer("Bill", "19872131", "DEF
Street", -32.1m));
customers.Add(new Customer("Carl", "29812371", "GHI
Street", -12.2m));
customers.Add(new Customer("David", "78612312", "JKL
Street", 12.6m));
```

Now suppose we want to search for all customers with negative account balances, we can use the following LINQ query.

```
var overdue =
    from cust in customers
    where cust.Balance < 0
    orderby cust.Balance ascending
    select new { cust.Name, cust.Balance };
```

This query is similar to the first query, with two main differences. Here, we used two additional keywords, `orderby` and `ascending`, to arrange the results in ascending order.

In addition, we used the `new` keyword in the select statement. The `new` keyword is needed whenever we want to select more than one field from the objects.

To execute and print the results, we can use the `foreach` loop below:

```
foreach (var cust in overdue)
    Console.WriteLine("Name = {0}, Balance = {1}",
cust.Name, cust.Balance);
```

We will get

```
Name = Bill, Balance = -32.1
Name = Carl, Balance = -12.2
```

Chapter 11: File Handling

Cool! We've come to the last chapter of the book before the project. In this chapter, we'll learn how to read and write to an external file.

In Chapter 5 previously, we learned how to get input from users using the `ReadLine()` method. However, in some cases, getting users to enter data into our program may not be practical, especially if our program needs to work with large amounts of data. In cases like this, a more convenient way is to prepare the needed information as an external file and get our programs to read the information from the file.

C# provides us with a number of classes to work with files. The classes that we are going to look at in this chapter are the `File`, `StreamWriter` and `StreamReader` classes. All three classes are available in the `System.IO` namespace. To use the methods in this chapter, you have to add the directive

```
using System.IO;
```

to the start of your code.

Reading a Text File

To read data from a text file, we use the `StreamReader` class.

Suppose we want to read data from the file "myFile.txt" located on the C drive. The example below shows how to do it.

```
1 string path = "c:\\myFile.txt";
2 using (StreamReader sr = new StreamReader(path))
3 {
4    while (sr.EndOfStream != true)
5    {
6        Console.WriteLine(sr.ReadLine());
7    }
8
9    sr.Close();
```

```
10 }
```

On line 1, we first declare a `string` variable `path` and assign the path of the file to the variable.

```
string path = "c:\\myFile.txt";
```

Note that we have to use double slashes \\ when writing the path. This is because if we only use a single slash, the compiler will think the single slash is the beginning of an escape sequence and interpret \m as an escape sequence. This will result in an error.

On line 2, we create a `StreamReader` instance. The `StreamReader` constructor takes in one argument – the path of the file to be read.

```
StreamReader sr = new StreamReader(path)
```

Notice that we create this `StreamReader` instance inside a pair of parenthesis that follows the word `using` on line 2?

The `using` keyword here is different from the one that we use when writing a directive.

The `using` keyword here ensures that the `Dispose()` method is always called. The `Dispose()` method is a pre-written method in the `System` namespace that closes or releases any unmanaged resources such as files and streams once they are no longer needed. When we use the `using` keyword, we ensure that the `Dispose()` method is called even if an exception occurs and prevents our code from reaching Line 9 where we manually close the file. It is good practice to always use the `using` keyword whenever you are dealing with files. The code to read and close the file is enclosed within curly braces { } after the `using` statement.

From lines 4 to 7, we use a `while` loop to read the text file line by line.

```
while (sr.EndOfStream != true)
{
    Console.WriteLine(sr.ReadLine());
}
```

`EndOfStream` is a property of the `StreamReader` class that returns `true` when the end of the file is reached. As long as the end of file is not reached, the `while` loop will continue to run.

Inside the `while` loop, we have the statement

```
Console.WriteLine(sr.ReadLine());
```

`sr.ReadLine()` reads a line from the text file and returns it as a string. This string is then printed onto the screen using the `Console.WriteLine()` method.

Finally, after we finish reading the file, we close the file so that other programs may use it. You should always close your file once you no longer need it.

```
sr.Close();
```

That's it. That's how you read a text file in C#. Pretty straightforward right?

However, there is one problem with the code above. This code will generate an error if the file "myFile.txt" cannot be found. We have two options here.

Option 1: try...catch

The first option is to use a `try...catch` statement as shown below:

```
1 try
2 {
3   using (StreamReader sr = new StreamReader(path))
4   {
5       while (!sr.EndOfStream)
6       {
7           Console.WriteLine(sr.ReadLine());
8       }
9       sr.Close();
10  }
11 }catch (FileNotFoundException e)
```

```
12 {
13  Console.WriteLine(e.Message);
14 }
```

From lines 1 to 11, we try to open, read and close the file in the `try` block.

From lines 11 to 14, we use a `catch` block to catch the `FileNotFoundException` exception if the file is not found. Inside the `catch` block, we print an error statement to inform users that the file is not found.

Option 2: File.Exists()

The second method to deal with a "file not found" scenario is to use the `Exists()` method in the `File` class. As the name suggests, the `Exists()` method checks if a file exists. The `File` class is a pre-written class in the `System.IO` namespace that provides static methods for the creation, copying, deletion, moving, and opening of a single file.

To use the `Exists()` method, we use an `if` statement to check if the file exists before using a `StreamReader` to open and read the file.

```
if (File.Exists(path))
{
    using (StreamReader sr = new StreamReader(path))
    {
        while (!sr.EndOfStream)
        {
            Console.WriteLine(sr.ReadLine());
        }
        sr.Close();
    }
}else
{
    //Do something else
}
```

In the `else` block, we can write code to create the file if it is not found.

As you can see, the two methods for dealing with cases where the file is missing are quite similar. However, the `File.Exists()` method is the preferred method as it is faster than the `try...catch` statement.

Writing to a Text File

Next, let us look at how to write to a text file.

To write to a text file, we use the `StreamWriter` class.

If you want to append data to an existing file, you create a `StreamWriter` instance like this

```
StreamWriter sw = new StreamWriter(path, true);
```

where `path` is the path of the file and `true` indicates that we want to append the data.

If you want to overwrite any existing data in the file, you create a `StreamWriter` instance like this

```
StreamWriter sw = new StreamWriter(path);
```

When we create the `StreamWriter` instance, the constructor looks for the file at the given path. If the file is not found, it creates the file.

After we instantiate our `StreamWriter` object, we can start writing to our file using the `WriteLine()` method as shown below:

```
sw.WriteLine("It is easy to write to a file.");
```

After we finish writing to the file, we have to close the file by writing

```
sw.Close();
```

Note that when you write to a text file, it is also good practice to enclose your code in a `using` statement. The code below shows a complete example of how all these come together.

```csharp
using System;
using System.Collections.Generic;
using System.Linq;
using System.Text;
using System.Threading.Tasks;
using System.IO;

namespace FileDemo
{
    class Program
    {
        static void Main(string[] args)
        {
            //declaring the path to the file
            string path = "myfile.txt";

            //Writing to the file
            using(StreamWriter sw=new
        StreamWriter(path, true))
            {
                sw.WriteLine("ABC");
                sw.WriteLine("DEF");
                sw.Close();
            }

            //Reading from the file
            if (File.Exists(path))
            {
                using(StreamReader sr=new
            StreamReader(path))
                {
                    while (!sr.EndOfStream)
                    {
                        Console.WriteLine(sr.
                    ReadLine());
                    }
                    sr.Close();
                }
            }
            Console.Read();
        }
```

```
        }
    }
```

In this example, we choose to append data to our file when we write to it.
When you run this program for the first time, you will get

```
ABC
EFG
```

as the file output and screen display. If you run it for the second time,
you will get

```
ABC
EFG
ABC
EFG
```

As the full path of "myfile.txt" is not given in this example, the text file will
be created in the same folder as the .exe file, which is in the FileDemo >
FileDemo > Debug > Bin folder.

Project – A Simple Payroll Software

Congratulations!

We have now completed the core concepts in C#. In this final chapter, we are going to get our feet wet by coding a complete console application that generates the salary slips of a small company.

Ready?

Overview

First, let's create a new console application and name it `CSProject`.

This application consists of six classes as shown below.

```
Staff
Manager : Staff
Admin : Staff
FileReader
PaySlip
Program
```

The `Staff` class contains information about each staff in the company. It also contains a virtual method called `CalculatePay()` that calculates the pay of each staff.

The `Manager` and `Admin` classes inherit the `Staff` class and override the `CalculatePay()` method.

The `FileReader` class contains a simple method that reads from a .txt file and creates a list of `Staff` objects based on the contents in the .txt file.

The `PaySlip` class generates the pay slip of each employee in the company. In addition, it also generates a summary of the details of staff who worked less than 10 hours in a month.

Finally, the `Program` class contains the `Main()` method which acts as the main entry point of our application.

The Staff Class

First, let's start with the `Staff` class. The `Staff` class contains basic information about an employee and provides a method for calculating basic pay. It serves as a parent class from which two other classes will be derived.

Fields

This class has one `private float` field called `hourlyRate` and one `private int` field called `hWorked`. Try declaring these fields yourself.

Properties

Next, declare three `public` auto-implemented properties for the class. The properties are `TotalPay`, `BasicPay` and `NameOfStaff`.

`TotalPay` is a `float` property and has a `protected` setter. `BasicPay` is a `float` property and has a `private` setter. `NameOfStaff` is a `string` property and has a `private` setter. The getters of all three properties are `public`. Hence, you do not need to declare the access modifiers of these getters as they have the same access level as the properties.

In addition to these three auto-implemented methods, the `Staff` class also has a `public` property called `HoursWorked`. The backing field for this property is the `hWorked` field.

This property has a getter that simply returns the value of `hWorked`. The setter checks if the value set for `HoursWorked` is greater than 0. If it is, it assigns `value` to `hWorked`. If it is not, it assigns 0 to `hWorked`. Try declaring this property yourself. You can refer to Chapter 7 for help.

Constructor

The Staff class has a public constructor with two parameters, name (string) and rate (float). Inside the constructor, we assign the two parameters to the property NameOfStaff and the field hourlyRate respectively. Try coding this constructor yourself.

Method

Now, let's write the methods for the class.

First, we'll code a virtual method called CalculatePay().

CalculatePay() is public, has no parameters and does not return a value. The method does three things:

First, it prints the line "Calculating Pay..." on the screen. Next, it assigns the value of hWorked*hourlyRate to the BasicPay property. Finally, it assigns the value of BasicPay to the TotalPay property. In other words, BasicPay and TotalPay will have the same value. Try coding this method yourself.

Finally, write a ToString() method to display the values of the fields and properties of the Staff class. That's all there is to the Staff class.

The table below shows a summary of the Staff class.

Fields

```
private float hourlyRate
private int hWorked (backing field for HoursWorked)
```

Properties

```
public float TotalPay
public float BasicPay
public string NameOfStaff
public int HoursWorked
```

Constructor

```
public Staff(string name, float rate)
```

Methods

```
public virtual void CalculatePay()
public override string ToString()
```

The Manager : Staff Class

Next, let's move on to code the Manager class.

Fields

The Manager class is a child class of the Staff class. It has one private const field called managerHourlyRate that is of float type. Try declaring this field and initializing it with a value of 50.

Properties

Manager also has a public auto-implemented property called Allowance. Allowance is of int type and has a private setter. Try coding this property.

Constructor

Now, let's declare the constructor for Manager. The Manager class has a public constructor with a string parameter, name.

The task of the constructor is to call the base constructor and pass the parameter name and the field managerHourlyRate to the base constructor. Other than that, the child constructor does nothing. Hence, there is nothing within the curly braces of the child constructor. Try coding this constructor yourself. You can refer to the Manager class summary below for help if you have problems coding the constructor.

Method

Next, let's code a method to override the `CalculatePay()` method in the `Staff` class. As `Manager` is derived from `Staff`, it has access to the `BasicPay`, `TotalPay` and `HoursWorked` properties declared in the `Staff` class.

In addition, `Manager` also has its own property – `Allowance`. We'll be making use of these four properties in this method.

First, let's declare the method. `CalculatePay()` is `public` and does not return any value. We have to use the `override` keyword when declaring this method as it overrides the `CalculatePay()` method in the `Staff` class.

Within the `CalculatePay()` method in the `Manager` class, we shall first call the `CalculatePay()` method in the parent class and use it to set the values of `BasicPay` and `TotalPay`. To call a virtual method in the parent class, you have to use the `base` keyword. Add the following line to your `CalculatePay()` method.

```
base.CalculatePay();
```

This calls the `CalculatePay()` method in the base (parent) class, which sets the values of `BasicPay` and `TotalPay`. After setting the values of these two properties, let's go on to set the value of `Allowance`. We'll set the value to 1000.

Next, we want to change the value of `TotalPay`. Based on the `CalculatePay()` method in the base class, `TotalPay` is equal to `BasicPay`, both of which are equal to the product of `hWorked` and `hourlyRate`.

However, in the `Manager` child class, we want to update the value of `TotalPay` by adding an allowance to it. Suppose a manager is paid an allowance of $1000 if he/she worked more than 160 hours within that month. Try using an `if` statement to update the value of `TotalPay` based on the value of `HoursWorked`.

After updating the value of `TotalPay`, the `CalculatePay()` method is complete.

Finally, we need to code the `ToString()` method for the `Manager` class. Try coding this method.

Once you are done, the `Manager` class is complete. The table below shows a summary of the `Manager` class.

Fields

```
private const float managerHourlyRate
```

Properties

```
public int Allowance
```

Constructor

```
public Manager(string name) : base(name, managerHourlyRate)
```

Methods

```
public override void CalculatePay()
public override string ToString()
```

The Admin : Staff Class

The next class is the `Admin` class which is also derived from the `Staff` class.

Fields

The `Admin` class has two `private const` fields: `overtimeRate` and `adminHourlyRate`. Both fields are of `float` type. Try declaring these two fields and initializing them with the values 15.5 and 30 respectively.

Property

Next, try declaring a `public` auto-implemented property, `Overtime`.

`Overtime` is of `float` type and has a `private` setter.

Constructor

Now, let's declare the constructor. Similar to the constructor of the `Manager` class, the constructor of the `Admin` class is `public` and has one `string` parameter, `name`. Its job is to simply call the base constructor and pass the parameter `name` and the field `adminHourlyRate` to the base constructor.

Method

Finally, we are ready to code the `CalculatePay()` method for the `Admin` class. The `CalculatePay()` method in the `Admin` class is very similar to the method in the `Manager` class. Let's first declare the method.

Next, within the curly braces, we use the `CalculatePay()` method of the base class to set the `BasicPay` and `TotalPay` properties of an admin staff.

After setting the values of these two properties, we check if `HoursWorked` is greater than 160. If it is, we'll update the value of the `TotalPay` property.

Suppose an admin staff is paid an overtime pay on top of the basic pay if he/she worked more than 160 hours. Try using an `if` statement to update the `TotalPay` property of an admin staff.

The overtime pay is calculated with the following formula

`Overtime = overtimeRate * (HoursWorked - 160);`

where `overtimeRate` is a `private` field in the `Admin` class and

`Overtime` is a property in the same class. `HoursWorked` is a property inherited from the `Staff` class.

Done?

Great! Now, go on to code the `ToString()` method. With that, the `Admin` class is complete. The table below shows a summary of the class.

Fields

```
private const float overtimeRate
private const float adminHourlyRate
```

Properties

```
public float Overtime
```

Constructor

```
public Admin(string name) : base(name,
adminHourlyRate)
```

Methods

```
public override void CalculatePay()
public override string ToString()
```

The FileReader Class

Now, we are ready to code the `FileReader` class. The `FileReader` class is relatively straightforward.

It consists of one `public` method called `ReadFile()` that has no parameter. The method returns a list of `Staff` objects. The method declaration is as follows:

```
public List<Staff> ReadFile()
{

}
```

The `ReadFile()` method reads from a .txt file that consists of the names and positions of the staff. The format is:

```
Name of Staff, Position of Staff
```

An example is:

```
Yvonne, Manager
Peter, Manager
John, Admin
Carol, Admin
```

The name of the text file is "staff.txt" and is stored in the same folder as the .exe file. Create this file yourself using Notepad and store it in the CSProject > CSProject > Bin > Debug folder where the .exe file is located.

Now, we can start coding the `ReadFile()` method. We first declare four local variables named `myStaff`, `result`, `path` and `separator` as shown below.

```
List<Staff> myStaff = new List<Staff>();
string[] result = new string[2];
string path = "staff.txt";
string[] separator = {", "};
```

Next, we check if the file "staff.txt" exists using an `if` statement and the `File.Exists()` method. You need to add the directive

```
using System.IO;
```

in order to use the `File.Exists()` method.

If the file exists, we use a `StreamReader` object to read the text file line by line. (Refer to Chapter 11 if you need help with this.) Each time we read a line, we use the `Split()` method (refer to Chapter 4) to split the line into two parts and store the result in the `result` array. For instance, when we read the first line, the `Split()` method splits it into two strings "Yvonne" and "Manager". Hence, `result[0]` = `"Yvonne"` and `result[1]` = `"Manager"`.

Based on the value of `result[1]`, we use an `if` statement to create a `Manager` object if the value of `result[1]` is "Manager" or an `Admin` object if the value is "Admin". We add these objects to the list `myStaff`.

After we finish reading the file, we close the file using the `Close()` method.

If the file does not exist, we display a message to inform users of the error.

Finally, we return the list `myStaff` to the caller after the `if-else` statement.

That's all there is to the `FileReader` class. We do not need to declare a constructor for this class. We'll just use the default constructor that C# creates for us automatically. The summary for the `FileReader` class is shown below:

Methods

```
public List<Staff> ReadFile()
```

The PaySlip Class

Now, let's code the `PaySlip` class. This class is slightly different from the other classes we've seen so far. In addition to having fields, properties, methods and constructors, the `PaySlip` class also has an enum called `MonthsOfYear`.

Fields

First, let's declare the fields. The class has two `private int` fields named `month` and `year`. Try declaring them.

Enum

Next, we shall declare an enum named `MonthsOfYear` inside the `PaySlip` class. `MonthsOfYear` represents the twelve months of the year, where `JAN = 1`, `FEB = 2` etc. Try declaring this enum yourself. You do not need to specify any access modifier for this enum. An enum declared inside a class is `private` by default.

Constructor

Now, try adding a constructor to the `PaySlip` class. The constructor is `public` and has two `int` parameters `payMonth` and `payYear`. Inside the constructor, we assign the two parameters to the `private` fields `month` and `year` respectively.

Methods

Next, let us code the `GeneratePaySlip()` method. This method takes in a list of `Staff` objects and does not return anything. The method declaration is

```
public void GeneratePaySlip(List<Staff> myStaff)
{
}
```

Inside the method, we declare a `string` variable called `path`. Next, still within the `GeneratePaySlip()` method, we use a `foreach` loop to loop through the elements in `myStaff`. This can be done as follows:

```
foreach (Staff f in myStaff)
{
}
```

Everything that follows from here for the `GeneratePaySlip()` method is to be coded within the curly braces of the `foreach` loop.

First, we assign a value to the `path` variable based on the name of the staff.

Recall that the `Staff` class has a property called `NameOfStaff`?

Suppose `NameOfStaff` = "Yvonne", we want to assign the string "Yvonne.txt" to the `path` variable.

How would you do that? Try coding it yourself. (Hint: You can use `f.NameOfStaff` to access the staff's name and use the + operator to concatenate the ".txt" extension)

After assigning a value to `path`, we want to instantiate a `StreamWriter` object to write to the file at the path specified by the `path` variable, overwriting any existing content on the file so that each pay slip generated does not contain content from the previous month. Refer to Chapter 11 if you have forgotten how to use the `StreamWriter` class. Let's call the `StreamWriter` object `sw`.

We can then proceed to use a series of `sw.WriteLine()` statements to generate the pay slip of each employee.

A typical payslip for a manager looks like this:

```
1   PAYSLIP FOR DEC 2010
2   ==========================
3   Name of Staff: Yvonne
4   Hours Worked: 1231
5
6   Basic Pay: $61,550.00
7   Allowance: $1,000.00
8
9   ==========================
10  Total Pay: $62,550.00
11  ==========================
```

The numbers on the left are added for reference and are not part of the actual pay slip.

A typical payslip for an admin staff looks similar except for line 7. For an admin staff, line 7 will read something like:

```
Overtime Pay: $1,286.50
```

Let us now look at how to generate this payslip.

To write line 1, we need to access the `month` and `year` fields in the class. As `month` is an integer, we need to cast it into a `MonthsOfYear` enum value so that it will be written as `DEC` instead of `12`. The statement below shows how line 1 can be written.

```
sw.WriteLine("PAYSLIP FOR {0} {1}",
(MonthsOfYear)month, year);
```

Line 2 is easy to write. It is simply made up of a series of equal signs (=). Try coding it yourself.

To write lines 3 and 4, we need to access the `NameOfStaff` and `HoursWorked` properties in the `Staff` class. The statement below shows how it can be done for line 3.

```
sw.WriteLine("Name of Staff: {0}", f.NameOfStaff);
```

Try coding line 4 yourself.

Next, we use a `sw.WriteLine("");` statement to print an empty line.

To write line 6, we need to access the `BasicPay` property in the `Staff` class. In addition, we also need to use the `C` specifier to display the `BasicPay` property in currency notation (refer to Chapter 5). Try it yourself.

Line 7 is harder as we need to determine the runtime type of the current object in the `foreach` loop. We learned how to do that in Chapter 8. If the current instance is a `Manager` object, we access and print the

`Allowance` property in the `Manager` class. In order to access the `Allowance` property in the `Manager` class, we need to cast `f` into a `Manager` object by writing

`((Manager)f).Allowance`

If the current instance is an `Admin` object, we access and print the `Overtime` property in the `Admin` class. Try coding line 7 yourself. Line 8 is another empty line and line 9 is made up of a series of equal signs. Line 10 shows the total pay of the current staff, which we can get from the `TotalPay` property of the `Staff` class. Finally, line 11 is another line made up of equal signs. Try coding these lines yourself.

Last but not least, after generating the pay slip for each staff, we need to close the file using the `sw.Close()` method.

That brings us to the end of the `GeneratePaySlip()` method. Once you have finished coding this method, we can move on to the next method in the `PaySlip` class.

The next method generates a summary of employees who worked less than 10 hours in that month. Let's call this method `GenerateSummary()`.

Like the `GeneratePaySlip()` method, the `GenerateSummary()` method is `public`, takes in a list of `Staff` objects and does not return any value. Try declaring this method yourself.

Inside the `GenerateSummary()` method, we use LINQ to select all employees who worked less than 10 hours in that month. We want to know the `NameOfStaff` and `HoursWorked` properties for these employees. In addition, we want to arrange the result in ascending order based on `NameOfStaff`. Try coding this LINQ statement yourself and assigning the result to a `var` variable called `result`. You can refer to Chapter 10 for help.

Done?

Good.

Next, let us declare a string variable `path` and assign the string "summary.txt" to it.

Now we are ready to write to "summary.txt". Declare a `StreamWriter` instance to write to this file. A typical "summary.txt" file looks like this (numbers on the left are added for reference):

```
1    Staff with less than 10 working hours
2
3    Name of Staff: Carol, Hours Worked: 2
4    Name of Staff: Peter, Hours Worked: 6
```

Lines 1 and 2 should be quite easy to code. Try coding them yourself.

To print lines 3 and 4, we need to use a `foreach` loop to loop through each element in the `result` variable obtained from the LINQ statement. Try coding this yourself.

After displaying the result, you can close the "summary.txt" file using the `Close()` method.

That's it for our `GenerateSummary()` method.

After coding the `GenerateSummary()` method, we simply need to code the `ToString()` method and our `PaySlip` class is complete. The table below shows a summary of the `PaySlip` class.

Fields

```
private int month
private int year
```

Enum

```
enum MonthsOfYear
```

Constructor

```
public PaySlip(int payMonth, int payYear)
```

Methods

```
public void GeneratePaySlip(List<Staff> myStaff)
public void GenerateSummary(List<Staff> myStaff)
public override string ToString()
```

The Program Class

We've now come to the most important part of the project – the `Program` class. The `Program` class only has one method – the `Main()` method.

The Main() Method

First, let us declare four local variables for the `Main()` method. The first is a list of `Staff` objects. We shall call this list `myStaff`. The next is a `FileReader` object called `fr`. The remaining two are `int` variables. Let's call them `month` and `year` and initialize them to zero. Try declaring these local variables yourself.

Now, we shall use a `while` loop and a `try catch` statement to prompt users to input the year for the payslip. The loop will repeatedly prompt users to enter the year until it gets a valid value.

To do that, we use the `while` loop below:

```
1  while (year == 0)
2  {
3    Console.Write("\nPlease enter the year: ");
4
5    try
6    {
7        //Code to convert the input to an integer
8    }
9    catch (FormatException)
10   {
11       //Code to handle the exception
12   }
13 }
```

Inside the `try` block (Line 7), we read the value that the user entered and try to convert it to an integer. We then assign it to the variable `year`. If it is successful, `year` will no longer be zero and the `while` loop will exit. Try coding the `try` block yourself.

If the conversion is not successful, we catch the error in the `catch` block to prevent the program from crashing. Try coding an error message in the `catch` block (Line 11). When conversion is unsuccessful, `year` remains as zero and the `while` loop continues. Users will be repeatedly prompted to enter the year until they enter a valid value.

Once you are done with this `while` block, you can move on to code the `while` block to prompt users to enter the month. The `while` block for the `month` variable is very similar to the one for the `year` variable. However, we want to do more checks for the `month` variable.

In the `try` block, we first try to convert the input to an integer and assign it to the `month` variable. If it is successful, we use an `if` statement to check if `month` is less than 1 or greater than 12. If it is, the input is invalid. We'll display an error message to inform users that they have entered an invalid value. In addition, we'll also reset `month` to zero so that the `while` loop will repeat itself. Try coding this `try` block yourself.

After coding the `try` block, you can proceed to code the `catch` block which simply informs users of the error.

Done? Good.

Next, we shall add items to our `myStaff` list. We do that by using the `fr` object to call the `ReadFile()` method in the `FileReader` class and assigning the result to `myStaff`.
We can then start to calculate the pay for each staff. We'll use the following `for` loop for this.

```
for (int i = 0; i < myStaff.Count; i++)
{
    try
    {
    }
```

```
     catch (Exception e)
     {
     }
}
```

Within the `for` loop, we use a `try catch` statement. In the `try` block, we do the following:

First, prompt the user to enter the number of hours worked for each staff. An example of a prompt is

```
Enter hours worked for Yvonne:
```

where "Yvonne" is the name of the staff. You need to access the `NameOfStaff` property for each staff by writing `myStaff[i].NameOfStaff`.

Next, read the input, try to convert it to an integer and assign it to the `HoursWorked` property of the `Staff` object.

After that, we call the `CalculatePay()` method on the `Staff` object to calculate the pay of that staff.

Finally, we use the `ToString()` method to get information about the `Staff` object and display this information on the screen using the `Console.WriteLine()` method.

Try coding this `try` block yourself.

Next in the `catch` block, we try to catch any errors that might occur. Within this `catch` block, we simply display an error message and reduce the value of i by one (`i--;`) so that the `for` loop will iterate again for the current `Staff` object instead of moving on to the next element in `myStaff`.

Try coding this `catch` block yourself.

With that, we've come to the end of the `for` loop. We are now ready to generate the pay slips for each staff. To do that, we need to first declare and instantiate a `PaySlip` object. Let's call that object `ps`. We pass in the variables `month` and `year` to the constructor when instantiating the object.

Next, we use the `ps` object to invoke the `GeneratePaySlip()` and `GenerateSummary()` methods and pass in `myStaff` as the argument. Finally, we add a `Console.Read();` statement to prevent the console from closing immediately after the program ends.

Done?

If you have successfully coded the `Main()` program, give yourself a pat on the shoulders. You have just coded a complete program in C#! Well done!

If you have problems coding it, keep trying. You can refer to the suggested solution in Appendix A for reference.

Once you are done coding the `Main()` method, you are ready to run your program. Excited? Let's do it!

Click on the "Start" button to run the program and key in the values requested. The pay slips generated can be found in the same folder as the .exe file, which is in the CSProject > CSProject > Bin > Debug folder. Try making errors and keying in alphabetical letters instead of numbers. Play around with the program to see how it works. Does everything work as expected? If it does, great! You have done an excellent job! Try to think of ways to improve the software. For instance, you can include more checks to ensure that users entered the correct values for `year` and `HoursWorked`.

If your code does not work, compare it with the sample answer and try to figure out what went wrong. You'll learn a lot by analysing your mistakes. Problem solving is where the fun lies and where the reward is the greatest. Have fun and never give up! The sample answer can be found in Appendix A.

Thank You

We've come to the end of the book. Thank you for reading this book and I hope you have enjoyed the book. More importantly, I sincerely hope the book has helped you master the fundamentals of C# programming.

I know you could have picked from a dozen of books on C# programming, but you took a chance with this book. Thank you once again for downloading this book and reading all the way to the end. Please try the exercises and the project. You'll learn a lot by doing.

Now I'd like to ask for a "small" favor. Could you please take a minute or two to leave a review for this book on Amazon?

This feedback will help me tremendously and will help me continue to write more guides on programming. If you like the book or have any suggestions for improvement, please let me know. I will be deeply grateful. :)

Last but not least, remember you can download the source code for the project at http://www.learncodingfast.com/csharp.

You can also contact me at jamie@learncodingfast.com.

Appendix A – Project Answer

The source code for this program can be downloaded at
http://www.learncodingfast.com/csharp.

```
using System;
using System.Collections.Generic;
using System.Linq;
using System.Text;
using System.Threading.Tasks;
using System.IO;

namespace CSProject
{
    class Program
    {
        static void Main(string[] args)
        {
            List<Staff> myStaff = new List<Staff>();
            FileReader fr = new FileReader();
            int month = 0, year = 0;

            while (year == 0)
            {
                Console.Write("\nPlease enter the year: ");

                try
                {
                    year =
Convert.ToInt32(Console.ReadLine());
                }
                catch (Exception e)
                {
                    Console.WriteLine(e.Message + " Please
try again.");
                }
            }

            while (month == 0)
```

```csharp
            {
                Console.Write("\nPlease enter the month:
");

                try
                {
                    month =
Convert.ToInt32(Console.ReadLine());

                    if (month < 1 || month > 12)
                    {
                        Console.WriteLine("Month must be
from 1 to 12. Please try again.");
                        month = 0;
                    }
                }
                catch (Exception e)
                {
                    Console.WriteLine(e.Message + " Please
try again.");
                }
            }

            myStaff = fr.ReadFile();

            for (int i = 0; i< myStaff.Count; i++)
            {
                try
                {
                    Console.Write("\nEnter hours worked
for {0}: ", myStaff[i].NameOfStaff);
                    myStaff[i].HoursWorked =
Convert.ToInt32(Console.ReadLine());
                    myStaff[i].CalculatePay();

Console.WriteLine(myStaff[i].ToString());
                }
                catch (Exception e)
                {
                    Console.WriteLine(e.Message);
                    i--;
```

```csharp
            }
        }

        PaySlip ps = new PaySlip(month, year);
        ps.GeneratePaySlip(myStaff);
        ps.GenerateSummary(myStaff);

        Console.Read();
    }
}

class Staff
{
    private float hourlyRate;
    private int hWorked;

    public float TotalPay { get; protected set; }
    public float BasicPay { get; private set; }
    public string NameOfStaff { get; private set; }

    public int HoursWorked
    {
        get
        {
            return hWorked;
        }
        set
        {
            if (value > 0)
                hWorked = value;
            else
                hWorked = 0;
        }
    }

    public Staff(string name, float rate)
    {
        NameOfStaff = name;
        hourlyRate = rate;
    }
```

```csharp
        public virtual void CalculatePay()
        {
            Console.WriteLine("Calculating Pay...");

            BasicPay = hWorked * hourlyRate;
            TotalPay = BasicPay;
        }

        public override string ToString()
        {
            return "\nNameOfStaff = " + NameOfStaff
                + "\nhourlyRate = " + hourlyRate +
"\nhWorked = " + hWorked
                + "\nBasicPay = " + BasicPay +
"\n\nTotalPay = " + TotalPay;
        }
    }

    class Manager : Staff
    {
        private const float managerHourlyRate = 50;

        public int Allowance { get; private set; }

        public Manager(string name) : base(name,
managerHourlyRate) { }

        public override void CalculatePay()
        {
            base.CalculatePay();

            Allowance = 1000;

            if (HoursWorked > 160)
                TotalPay = BasicPay + Allowance;
        }

        public override string ToString()
        {
            return "\nNameOfStaff = " + NameOfStaff +
"\nmanagerHourlyRate = "
```

```csharp
            + managerHourlyRate + "\nHoursWorked = "
+ HoursWorked + "\nBasicPay = "
            + BasicPay + "\nAllowance = " + Allowance
+ "\n\nTotalPay = " + TotalPay;
        }
    }

    class Admin : Staff
    {
        private const float overtimeRate = 15.5f;
        private const float adminHourlyRate = 30f;

        public float Overtime { get; private set; }

        public Admin(string name) : base(name,
adminHourlyRate) { }

        public override void CalculatePay()
        {
            base.CalculatePay();

            if (HoursWorked > 160)
                Overtime = overtimeRate * (HoursWorked -
160);
        }

        public override string ToString()
        {
            return "\nNameOfStaff = " + NameOfStaff
            + "\nadminHourlyRate = " + adminHourlyRate +
"\nHoursWorked = " + HoursWorked
            + "\nBasicPay = " + BasicPay + "\nOvertime =
" + Overtime
            + "\n\nTotalPay = " + TotalPay;
        }
    }

    class FileReader
    {
        public List<Staff> ReadFile()
        {
```

```csharp
            List<Staff> myStaff = new List<Staff>();
            string[] result = new string[2];
            string path = "staff.txt";
            string[] separator = { ", " };

            if (File.Exists(path))
            {
                using (StreamReader sr = new
StreamReader(path))
                {
                    while (!sr.EndOfStream)
                    {
                        result =
sr.ReadLine().Split(separator,
StringSplitOptions.RemoveEmptyEntries);

                        if (result[1] == "Manager")
                            myStaff.Add(new
Manager(result[0]));
                        else if (result[1] == "Admin")
                            myStaff.Add(new
Admin(result[0]));
                    }
                    sr.Close();
                }
            }else
            {
                Console.WriteLine("Error: File does not
exist");
            }

            return myStaff;
        }
    }

    class PaySlip
    {
        private int month;
        private int year;
```

```
enum MonthsOfYear { JAN = 1, FEB = 2, MAR, APR,
MAY, JUN, JUL, AUG, SEP, OCT, NOV, DEC }

public PaySlip(int payMonth, int payYear)
{
    month = payMonth;
    year = payYear;
}

public void GeneratePaySlip(List<Staff>
myStaff)
{
    string path;

    foreach (Staff f in myStaff)
    {
        path = f.NameOfStaff + ".txt";

        using (StreamWriter sw = new
StreamWriter(path))
        {
            sw.WriteLine("PAYSLIP FOR {0} {1}",
(MonthsOfYear)month, year);
            sw.WriteLine("====================");
            sw.WriteLine("Name of Staff: {0}",
f.NameOfStaff);
            sw.WriteLine("Hours Worked: {0}",
f.HoursWorked);
            sw.WriteLine("");
            sw.WriteLine("Basic Pay: {0:C}",
f.BasicPay);

            if (f.GetType() == typeof(Manager))
                sw.WriteLine("Allowance: {0:C}",
((Manager)f).Allowance);
            else if (f.GetType() == typeof(Admin))
                sw.WriteLine("Overtime: {0:C}",
((Admin)f).Overtime);

            sw.WriteLine("");
            sw.WriteLine("====================");
```

```csharp
                    sw.WriteLine("Total Pay: {0:C}",
f.TotalPay);
                    sw.WriteLine("====================");

                    sw.Close();
            }
        }


    public void GenerateSummary(List<Staff>
myStaff)
        {
            var result
                = from f in myStaff
                  where f.HoursWorked < 10
                  orderby f.NameOfStaff ascending
                  select new { f.NameOfStaff,
f.HoursWorked };

            string path = "summary.txt";

            using (StreamWriter sw = new
StreamWriter(path))
            {
                sw.WriteLine("Staff with less than 10
working hours");
                sw.WriteLine("");

                foreach (var f in result)
                    sw.WriteLine("Name of Staff: {0},
Hours Worked: {1}", f.NameOfStaff, f.HoursWorked);

                sw.Close();
            }
        }

    public override string ToString()
        {
            return "month = " + month + "year = " +
year;
```

```
            }
        }
    }
```

Index

new, 121
newline, 45

O
object-oriented, 7, 70
overloading, 79
override, 80, 104, 107, 110

P
parameters, 77
params, 89
placeholders, 42
polymorphism, 102
private, 72, 111, 112
Program, 14, 71
properties, 28, 70, 73
protected, 94, 111, 113
public, 74, 111, 112

R
Read(), 13, 46
ReadLine(), 46
reference type, 37, 91, 118
Remove(), 36
RemoveAt(), 36
return, 74, 77, 78
run time, 105

S
setter, 74
signature, 79
Sort(), 30
Split(), 33

static, 85
StreamReader, 122, 125
StreamWriter, 122, 126
struct, 71, 116
Substring(), 32, 44
System, 12, 39, 47, 123
System.IO, 122, 125

T
tab, 45
ToDecimal(), 48
ToDouble(), 48
ToInt32(), 47, 69
ToSingle(), 48
ToString(), 80
try-catch-finally, 66
type casting, 26, 115, 142
typeof(), 105

U
using, 12, 123

V
value, 75
value type, 37, 91, 118
var, 120
virtual, 104
void, 77

W
Write(), 39
WriteLine(), 13, 39

Made in the USA
Middletown, DE
25 October 2017